The Astrology of

Makemake

Uranus' Higher Octave

Alan Clay
Melissa Billington

A Dwarf Planet University Publication

A Dwarf Planet University Publication
Copyright Alan Clay 2023

Artmedia
72 / 26 Antill St
Dickson ACT 2602
Australia
www.dwarfplanet.university
alan@artmedia.com.au

The Astrology of Makemake
Uranus' Higher Octave
ISBN: 978-0-6458033-1-0
ALL RIGHTS RESERVED

Cover image by astrologer, Karen La Puma
Author of the series, *A Toolkit for Awakening*
Karenlapuma.com

Contents

New Stars for a New Era

Many astrologers believe that new planets are discovered when we are ready to incorporate the new consciousness represented by that planet into our existing consciousness. We've noticed this with the discovery of Uranus, Neptune and Pluto over the last two hundred years. And with the discovery of ten more planets in the past twenty years, we're now entering a period of rapid consciousness development.

Our personal consciousness develops within the collective consciousness around us, and we see this personal consciousness mapped out in the personal planets in our chart. These are the planets out to Saturn that are visible to the naked eye, and they talk about facets of our personality that are important in living day-to-day.

When our consciousness is focussed on the inner planets, everything that is important is our feelings, our ideas and values, our agency and the luck and material rewards that these bring us. "You can't take it with you, right?" And at this level we tend not to be conscious of the action of the outer planets in our lives.

The inner planets represent aspects of personality, while the outer planets represent aspects of consciousness. As each new outer planet is discovered, it represents a new aspect of consciousness that is becoming available to us. The discovery of Uranus brought us intuitive consciousness, the discovery of Neptune, spiritual consciousness, and the discovery of Pluto, psychological consciousness.

So, the discovery of Makemake represents a new aspect of consciousness that we can now uncover in ourselves. Put simply, Makemake takes the intuitive understanding of Uranus and turns it into a rich contextual understanding, into a wisdom or a cosmic consciousness. However, this new consciousness doesn't kick in automatically, rather we must actively incorporate it into our lives.

Because these outer planets talk of consciousness, how they manifest in our lives depends on our current level of consciousness. Most people on Earth experience the outer planets as unconscious influences and so are unable to be sensitive and adaptable to these esoteric new energies. At this level the outer planets are only perceived when, like Pluto, they barge into our lives in a confrontational way.

As we develop spiritually, however, and consciously on-board these new energies into our lives, they become like guides into new territory, offering us special skills or challenges, depending on the aspects in our chart. At this level, rather than unconscious influences, the outer planets become like a new super-consciousness.

Thus, the discovery of so many new outer planets at one time represents a feast of new consciousness that is now available to us. The enlightenment that was only available to select gurus and priests is now available to everyone. But just as the gurus had to practice devoutly to be able to handle this divine power, we also need to work to on-board these new energies consciously in our lives.

Physical and Orbital

One of the main ways we discern the meaning of new planets is to look at their physical and orbital characteristics. It tells us a lot about Saturn that he has 82 moons, 150 moon-like objects, and rings. The precision required for that speaks of his structuring and limiting principles. Uranus spins with East-West poles and rotates around the Sun in the opposite direction from most of the other planets, that's very bohemian.

Makemake is the second brightest dwarf planet. We know light is consciousness, and we relate brightness to being smart, so this tells us he talks about a richer awareness. He is believed to have an icy surface and a rocky core. His surface is like a photochemical laboratory, where the sun's radiation converts the ice into gases. This tells us that his actions are scientific, experimental, and practice based.

The raw material for this chemical reaction is methane ice, which is found on Earth as a gas. And the element of air represents ideas, so he takes crystalline ideas and plays with them experimentally to liberate the active components. By extension, in our lives, he encourages us in the alchemical process of breaking down existing ideas into their component parts and playfully putting them back together in new configurations.

His orbit is 309 Earth years which is 26 years longer than Haumea and 61 years more than Pluto. Orbits are cycles and longer cycles encompass more, offering more growth potential. One day on Makemake is 7.77 Earth hours, so he refreshes faster, but over a longer time period, giving us greater opportunities to develop consciousness and refresh our spirit.

All the inner planets orbit the Sun in a plane called the ecliptic, which represents consensus reality. Much of our experience of the world is shaped by the unconscious agreements that we make about how it works, and this is what we call our consensus reality. And all the dwarf planets cut through this ecliptic, some more strongly than others.

Makemake's inclination is 29 degrees, so he cuts through consensus reality almost twice as strongly as Pluto, with his 17 degrees. The dwarf planets have oblong orbits, and Makemake's closest point is beneath the ecliptic. So, while he spends some of his time in the underworld, the orientation of his orbit means that he spends more time out in our world, gaining a bird's view over that reality.

He appears red in the visible spectrum, and significantly redder than the surface of Eris. This color is due to the Sun's ions breaking down the ice on the surface. This is a space-weathering process, which is shared by the new outer-limit of the solar system, Sedna, and also the centaur, Pholus. The orbit of Pholus joins the orbits of Neptune and Saturn, so he talks about bringing spirit and illumination into matter. And Sedna talks about spiritual destiny at the highest level, so Makemake is also talking about illumination and spirituality.

In June of 2034 he will be as far from the Sun as he ever reaches in his orbit. This aphelion is the culmination of the current cycle and from that point we will be integrating the perspective that Makemake has brought us over the last 154 years. From the wider, and wiser view that we've been gaining, the alchemical work in the waning phase is to refine down to essences. Refining from expansive gases to crystalline structures, from ideas to putting them into reality. From amassing information into winnowing this into usable applications.

Myth

The myth behind the name of a new planet also tells us a lot about its astrological meaning. Myths transmit knowledge across time and culture, but they need interpretation for the new time and the new culture.

Makemake is named after the creator god of the people of Easter Island. He was the god of fertility and the chief god of the bird-man cult, which succeeded the era when the famous stone heads were carved. He drove flocks of migratory seabirds to the island and was responsible for the fertility of food plants and fowls.

Birds symbolize the life of the spirit, along with freedom, expansiveness, and keen vision, so Makemake drives spirit into our lives and opens us to see the bigger picture with a bird's-eye view. He gives us the eagle-eyed ability to see the big picture and also zoom in on the detail at the same time.

Like Easter Island in the vast Pacific Ocean, we are each a speck in the vast universe, and yet the spirit energies can find us and nourish us if we are devoted and in the natural rhythm. Makemake ensures we are in the right place at the right time if we are sensitive and trust in spirit.

The myth tells us:

After a while, Makemake thought of creating the man, who would be just like him, who would have a voice and speak like him. Makemake fertilized some stones but there was no result because the reflux waters ran

*over the extension of unproductive and bad land. He
fertilized the water and from the scattered semen only
many small paroko fishes came out. Finally, Makemake
fertilized the clay soil. Man was born from it. Makemake
saw that this turned out well.[1]*

Although Makemake is a male creation god, the feminine
isn't absent. Rather, the feminine is so present that it's
invisible because it's assumed as the backdrop to all that is.
In this myth the whole world is receptive and Makemake's
fertilization catalyses new life. Makemake helps us understand
that everything is an opportunity for creation. Our spirit
draws towards us the fertile opportunity to manifest our
consciousness in the real world.

In the myth, Makemake has an assistant as well as other
companion gods, so he is the master of an enterprise. Four
gods were associated with bringing the birds and each had a
servant god. Makemake's principal companion god was Haua,
another male. The invocation which accompanies an offering
to Makemake always includes Haua.

Makemake has no wife, but he does have children, so he
could be our first gay deity. Or he could be celibate. Either
way his spirit drive is not distracted by normal sexual
relationship games. Indeed, he encourages us to reimagine
gender, and since his discovery we have had an explosion in
gender identity consciousness. We see this expressed in the
widespread use of preferred pronouns.

In the myth Makemake was born of a skull belonging to an old
priestess. The sacred skull was washed out to sea with the
priestess in pursuit, and made landfall on another island.

Makemake and Haua were constant companions.

---

1   https://imaginarapanui.com/en/make-make-easter-island-god/

They fished and hunted all over the island. Makemake especially enjoyed having birds to eat, for there had been no birds on the island of Mataveri (Easter Island).

Makemake often shared his food with the old priestess. One day she asked him, "Why don't they have good food like this to eat back on our old island?" Makemake did not know the answer to this question. He asked Haua, "Why don't you and I chase some of the birds back to Mataveri? The people there would like them. They have no birds of their own to eat."

Makemake and Haua did just that. They rounded up a whole flock of sooty terns. They drove them across the ocean to Mataveri. Indeed the islanders were pleased. They thanked Makemake and Haua over and over. Then they ate the birds. The islanders did not use common sense. Before long, all of the birds were eaten and gone. They returned to their old diet of fish, hoping Makemake would return soon with more birds for them to eat.

A few years later, Makemake and Haua decided to check on Mataveri and see how the birds were doing. When they arrived, they could not find a single remaining bird. All the birds were gone. Makemake was puzzled. He and Haua rounded up another large flock of terns and drove them back to Mataveri. This time he instructed the islanders to allow them to lay eggs so there would be more birds for them to eat.

Soon the terns built many nests, and laid many eggs. The islanders were not sure what to make of all this. One day they discovered something wonderful. The eggs were good to eat! Now the islanders thanked

Makemake and Haua for both the birds and for the eggs. Then they ate them all. Every one. Every bird and every egg. Then they waited for Makemake to bring more.

"Well," said Makemake. "It has been a few years. What say, Haua. Shall we go back to my old island and see how our birds have done?" Haua agreed. They set off at once. When Makemake and Haua arrived on Mataveri they again found no trace of any birds. Makemake questioned the people sternly, "Didn't I tell you to allow them to lay eggs?"

"Oh we did," answered the people. "And we thank you for that because they were very delicious." "WHAT?" thundered Makemake. "You ATE the eggs?"

That evening Makemake and Haua puzzled over the problem. "First they ate the birds. Then they ate the eggs. These people just don't think! They don't understand anything about birds." Haua agreed. Then they had an idea. The very next day Makemake and Haua drove a third flock of sooty terns from Matriohiva. This time they put all the birds on Motu Nui. Motu Nui was an empty island just across the water from Mataveri. Here the birds could build their nests and raise their young. The men could capture and eat just a few of the birds at a time. The rest would be safe.[2]

This myth obviously teaches us to nurture the life cycle. We have to learn to think collectively, to understand the whole cycle of growth in which we are involved and upon which we rely, and to nurture each point of that cycle. Otherwise, we're

---

2   https://islandculturearchivalsupport.wordpress.com/2018/03/14/ makemake-and-the-birds-of-easter-island/

likely to be short-sighted and satiate ourselves in each moment at the expense of future generations of life. The eggs in the myth, when taken by themselves, are finite food sources. But when the eggs are nourished and encouraged to flourish into being by spirit, they then perpetuate the greater cycle of life.

Makemake swoops in and saves the people, by teaching them to understand the life cycle. And in our lives, he teaches us to swoop in and save ourselves by understanding where we are in our personal cycle. When we do, we realize how we can correct our behaviour, not only for our own benefit, but for the benefit of all beings.

Motu Nui and the Birdman Cult

So the birds thrived on the small island of Motu Nui, and from about 1500 to 1867 an annual ceremony took place which was based on the Makemake cult and served to determine the Bird-Man of the island.

> *Contestants, all men of importance, were revealed in the dreams of other islanders. Each contestant would appoint a man of lesser status who would swim to the island of Motu Nui and await the arrival of the birds, hoping to return with the first egg.*

> *The race was very dangerous, and many were killed by sharks, by drowning, or by falling from cliff faces. Once the first egg was collected, the finder would swim back with it secured in a reed basket tied to his forehead. He would climb the steep, rocky cliff face and, if he did not fall, present the egg to his patron.*

> *The new Bird-Man, who was the patron from the dream, went into seclusion for a year in a special ceremonial house to serve a mediating function between the inhabitants and the god Makemake. He*

was entitled to gifts of food and his clan had sole rights to collect that season's harvest of wild bird eggs from Motu Nui.[3]

This tells us that Makemake is competitive, best practice. We see the enterprise theme again with contestants appearing in others dreams and then appointing others to complete the challenge. So, he gives us an understanding of the complex interaction and teamwork required to get to any particular outcome.

3   https://en.wikipedia.org/wiki/Tangata_manu

Sabian Symbol for the Discovery Degree

The Sabian Symbols were channelled by clairvoyant Elsie Wheeler and astrologer Marc Edmund Jones, and they give us a rich visual symbols for each degree of the zodiac.

We can look at the degree of Makemake in his discovery chart like a birth moment, as the planet arrives in our consciousness. We'll look at his chart as a whole in a coming chapter, but first the Sabian Symbol for Makemake's placement gives us another pathway to interpret this new astrological energy.

The Sabian Symbol for Makemake's discovery is 21 degrees Virgo, which is:

A Girls' Basketball Team

Dane Rudhyar describes the keynote of this image as being:

Physical training as a means to inculcate the feeling of participation in a collective culture.

- *Here the players operate as a team.*

- *What should be stressed here is the formation of a group acting as an organic whole and training itself to operate in a social context.*

- *It implies the training for group integration of "girls," i.e. of a type of consciousness more specifically receptive to collective forces.*

So Makemake talks about training to be part of an organic whole where the participants are sensitive to one another and to their collective mission.

19

Similarly, Lynda Hill describes this symbol as:

Joining with others and working as a team to achieve common aspirations.

- *You may be into doing things by yourself, but you'll still have interactions with others who will mold how you do things and how you'll perform.*
- *There is a need to cooperate and play by the rules of the game to achieve your goals.*

So Makemake is talking about the context, which molds how our interactions will be received. If we are challenged by Makemake, we might lose sight of the bigger picture and not want to play by the rules or cooperate with others. Or we could indulge in backbiting and rivalry or try to hog the limelight. Whereas when we embrace his energy, we can joyfully participate in our lives, understanding the value of teamwork and the importance of training and practice.

Makemake as a Higher Octave

Another way of understanding these new outer planets is to look at them as a higher octave of an inner planet energy that we know well. The higher octave expresses the inner energy at a more spiritual level. However, the inner energy is not simply stepped up to the higher level, but rather the higher octave acts on the inner octave to repolarize that energy in our daily lives.

We can think of Makemake, a quick-witted, quasi-trickster who can give us a devotional focus bordering on genius, as the higher octave of Uranus. And Uranus is traditionally the higher octave of Mercury. We see the focus on mental ability and trickster tendencies in all three of these bodies.

If Mercury's ideas and communications are networked into the collective consciousness by Uranus, then Makemake talks about the culture or the nation that is addressed by that network. Makemake gives Uranus's intuitive impulses meaning and context which transforms our understanding of his unexpected ways. And Uranus's lateral web gives Mercury's detail an energetic network to organize and connect his information.

Typically, in modern Western astrology, we relate Uranus with astrology so, as his higher octave, Makemake must also relate to astrology. We can think of Uranus as the map of the planets, as the birth chart, and Makemake as the interpretation that a skilled practitioner can draw out of that symbol. And Mercury communicates the insights.

Astrologer Sue Kientz was the first to suggest that Makemake was the higher octave of Uranus in her ground-breaking book, *More Plutos*. And our research at the Dwarf Planet University strongly agrees.

Higher Octave Case Study

Now, if these three planets are higher octaves of one another, we would expect to find them singing in chorus in major events in our lives. Let's examine these three octaves in the chart of the father of computer science and artificial intelligence, Alan Turing, for the date that his seminal paper was received by the London Mathematical Society, May 28, 1936.

"Ladies will take their computers for walks."

Alan Turing was an English mathematician, cryptologist, and philosopher who worked for Britain's codebreaking centre during the Second World War. He is credited with formalising the concepts of algorithm and computation with his Turing Machine, which broke the German code. Some 80 years ago he predicted, *"One day ladies will take their computers for walks in the park and tell each other, 'My little computer said such a funny thing this morning.'"*

In his natal chart, Turing has Uranus conjunct his MC, with Makemake conjunct his ASC and Mercury in the 2nd house. Makemake is semisextile Mercury and trine Uranus, so the three octaves are actively aligned with each other and with the angles in his chart. On the day his seminal paper was received, transiting Uranus in the 12th was closely sextile his natal Mercury in the 2nd, and transiting Makemake was conjunct his Mercury, within 2 degrees. So, we can see right there, the resonance between these three planets.

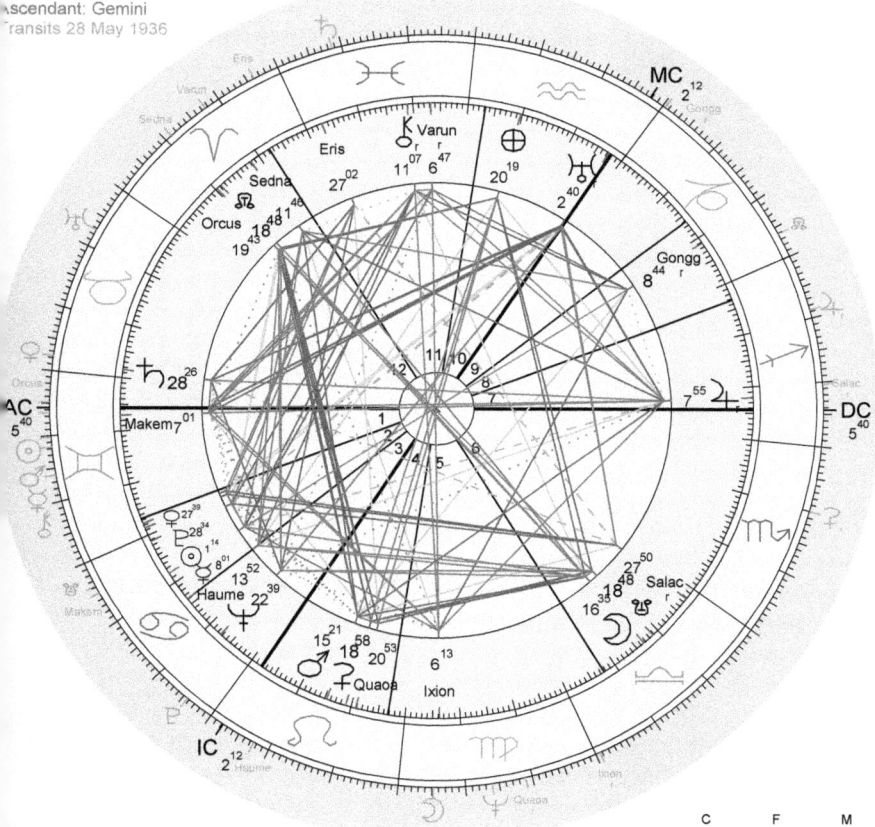

Name: ♂ Alan Turing [Adb]
born on Su., 23 June 1912
in London, ENG (UK)
0w10, 51n30

Time: 2:15 a.m.
Univ.Time: 2:15
Sid. Time: 20:17:52

ASTRO)DIENST
www.astro.com

Type: 2.GW 0.0-1 29-Sep-2023

Natal Chart (Method: Web Style / Placidus)
Sun sign: Cancer
Ascendant: Gemini
Transits 28 May 1936

	Natal		Transit
Sun	1 Can 13'51"		6 ♊ 29'
Moon	16 Lib 34'35"		5 ♍ 11'
Mercury	8 Can 0'49"		11 ♊ 46'
Venus	27 Gem 38'58"		27 ♉ 40'
Mars	15 Leo 21' 1"		10 ♓ 14'
Jupiter	7 Sag 54'38"r		21 ♏ 18'r
Saturn	28 Tau 26'12"		21 ♓ 26'
Uranus	2 Aqu 39'58"r		7 ♉ 17'
Neptune	22 Can 39'25"		13 ♍ 59'r
Pluto	28 Gem 33'51"		25 ♋ 40'
True Node	18 Ari 48'11"d		5 ♌ 50'r
Mean T.Node	18 Lib 48'11"d		5 ♌ 57'r
Chiron	11 Pis 6'50"r		19 ♓ 11'
⊕ Fort.	20 Aqu 18'58"		(Kilt)Ω
Ceres	13 Leo 58' 9"		19 ♍ 50'
08 Haumea	13 Can 52'22"		7 ♋ 31'
2 Makemake	7 Gem 0'46"		6 ♋ 4'
88 Gonggong	8 Cap 44'10"r		20 ♑ 33'r
47 Salacia	27 Lib 49'33"r		9 ♏ 35'
99 Eris	27 Pis 2'18"		0 ♈ 40'
78 Ixion	6 Vir 13' 2"		8 ♍ 55'
82 Orcus	19 Ari 43' 9"		4 ♉ 51'
10 Quaoar	20 Leo 52'50"		18 ♍ 59'r
77 Sedna	11 Ari 46'10"		19 ♈ 0'
90 Varuna	8 Pis 47'28"r		12 ♈ 25'

5 Gem 39' 42' | 2: 28 Gem 45' | 3: 13 Can 52'
2 Aqu 12' 1" | 11: 26 Aqu 49' | 12: 7 Ari 38'

	C	F	M
F	♎ OrSe	♂ ? Qu	♃
A	☽ ♉ Sa	♓ ⊕ MC	♀ ♇ Ma ♈ AC
E	Go	♄	Ix
W	☉ ☿ ♆ Ha		⚷ ErVa

23

Transiting North Lunar Node in the 8th house of shared energies and resources was semisextile his natal Uranus–MC conjunction, reiterating the reception of his paper as a fateful turning point in his life. Transiting Mercury in the 1st was also sextile his natal Sedna, the planet that rules AI, in his 12th house of institutions. At the same time, Uranus was transiting through his 12th house, sextile his natal Mercury and semi-sextile his Makemake, thus activating both of the other octaves.

Uranus was also transiting sextile his natal Varuna, the planet of sovereignty, in the 11th house of collective consciousness. Intriguingly, Makemake, transiting his 2nd house of material reality, was also trine his natal Varuna that day. We can think of Varuna as the higher octave of Saturn, signifying the notability we derive from having an impact. And here we see both the higher octaves making flowing aspects with his natal Varuna, predicting the fame his breakthrough would bring.

The importance of Makemake is especially emphasized with transiting Sun in the 1st house closely conjunct his natal Makemake and transiting Makemake conjunct his natal 2nd-house Sun within 3 degrees. Makemake was also transiting closely sesquiquadrate his Part of Fortune, semisextile his ASC, and conjunct his Mercury within 2 degrees, with the conjunction becoming exact over the next few years as he realized his seminal ideas. So, we clearly see the resonance between these three planets.

Discovery Events

Another way we can infer the meaning of new planets is to look at events around the time of their discovery which give us an understanding of the astrological energy of the planet. Makemake was discovered on 31 March 2005.

Launch of YouTube

The first discovery event we link Makemake with is YouTube's launch on Valentine's Day, 14 February 2005. Mercury is communications and Uranus is unity in diversity. Makemake makes the individual universal and also brings the universal into our personal world. Similarly, YouTube operates as a medium for individual expression that is then available worldwide with the most popular material democratically elevated to the top.

Moving from the individual expression of self with Mercury, and then influenced by Uranus's Aquarian inclusion of all, Makemake then expands this out to make even the smallest voice visible and available on the largest level.

Nonstop Earth Circumnavigation

Another discovery event we link with Makemake is Steve Fossett's nonstop circumnavigation of the Earth in a fixed-wing aircraft over 3 days, from 28 February to 3 March, 2005. This landmark achievement is a profound example of biomimicry of bird's flight. Seeing the whole earth in one go symbolises Makemake's bigger spiritual view of our world.

Brain Breakthrough

We also link Makemake with a brain breakthrough reported in LiveScience on 25 March 2005.

> *Your brain cells change channels sort of like a television, scientists say. Specific cells in the noggin can change what they allow through their membranes by swapping one kind of channel, or membrane opening, for another. This lets your brain fine-tune messages and adjust connections to control fine motor skills.*
>
> *A brain cell's activity level depends on its neighbours - the nerves and other cells that connect to it. They don't physically touch, but a cell and its neighbour are close enough that molecules released from one can travel directly to the next. These molecules dock at specific receptors on the cell's membrane and trigger the opening of gate-like channels. Depending on the receptor and the channel, sodium, calcium, chloride, or other charged atoms will flow into the cell.[4]*

This tells us that Makemake consciousness involves a sifting of the building blocks of ideas, and of the endless possibilities for recombining those ideas, allowing a greater understanding. This mimics the planet's alchemical process of breaking down crystalline ideas into their component parts.

On a bigger scale, our individual Makemake activity level depends on the culture in which we are living. Our interaction with that culture triggers the release of ideas, which travel directly between members and, when they connect, open gate-like channels which enable us to participate in a larger story. As we develop our Makemake we are able to fine-tune these

---

4   https://www.livescience.com/6929-brain-channels.html

messages and adjust our connections to influence how they are received.

Google Earth Launched

Publicly launched in June 2005, Google Earth is a program which renders a 3 dimensional representation of the Earth based on satellite imagery.

> Google Earth is a unique geomapping and tagging program that uses composite imagery to form a comprehensive, interactive map of the Earth. By stitching together more than a billion satellite and aerial images, the application provides a versatile tool that allows individuals and groups to track climate change, discover unknown geographic and ecological features, and record our history.
>
> This digital cartography tool continues to be a useful resource for governments, private organizations and individuals who want to track and tag geographic data to myriad ends. By collecting and curating enormous amounts of data, Google has made it possible for conservationists to observe the shifting patterns of flora and fauna on a global scale, for governments to observe the growth of cities worldwide, and for individuals to tell their personal stories in a unique way.[5]

Makemake gives us the ability to take the big satellite view of our reality, and drill down anywhere to discover finer and finer detail. Each level holds more information, enabling us to collect and curate this data into a rich understanding. And the richer our understanding becomes, the better able we are to tell our story in a unique way.

---

5   https://www.livescience.com/65504-google-earth.html

The Cardboard Box

And finally, 2005 was the year that the cardboard box was inducted into the National Toy Hall of Fame. Children will often play with the box that the new toy comes in, more than the toy itself, because it offers a broader field for the imagination. The induction of the cardboard box into the Toy Hall of Fame talks about Makemake's playfulness and curiosity.

The more we can approach the big picture from an open and childlike perspective, and see the context as just as valuable as the content, the more we will be able to embrace our Makemake consciousness and make cosmic sense out of the experiences in our lives.

Discovery Chart Interpretation

Another way that we can understand these new planets is to look at the chart for the planet's discovery. Makemake was discovered on 31 March 2005 and, in the chart for that day, Makemake is in Virgo. We don't have a discovery time so we can't look at the house, however, the Virgo placement is again talking about seeing the big picture in the smallest detail.

Makemake is inconjunct no-nonsense Eris, which is conjunct with his North Node in Aries. Eris is the higher octave of Pluto and she turns life into love and opens everything to the light. The conjunction with the node means Makemake is encouraging us to look fully at our experiences, and we'll get best results in understanding the big picture when we embrace our dharma with an unflinching gaze and a fierce grace that leaves no detail out.

This conjunction forms a grand fire trine with his Moon conjunct Pluto in Sagittarius and his Orcus in Leo. Moon conjunct Pluto has a similar quality to Eris in Aries, cutting through our personal feelings to reveal the bigger perspective that we need in order to transform our understanding of ourselves. And the grand trine between these conjunctions and Orcus in Leo, tells us that when we embrace Makemake, everything that we discover becomes a valuable, creative resource for our growth.

Orcus is Pluto's new straight-talking brother, who is able to transmute shadow into light at the top level. He is also in a sesquiquadrate with an exact conjunction of the Sun and

Venus in Aries. This conjunction strongly emphasizes the importance of values in our exploration of the big picture, and the sesquiquadrate with Orcus challenges us to see the shadow in a positive way, so we can act in the face of potential despair. This ability to 'see things as they are' might otherwise get lost in the grand trine vortex, but instead the sesquiquadrate motivates progress.

There is also an opposition from Orcus to Gonggong, who is an empathic wizard at the top level. This opposition highlights our need to transmute shadow into light in our big picture research, by lifting our energy out of self-indulgence so we can actively empathize with others. Gonggong is in the last few minutes of Aquarius, which indicates that Makemake can bring us a really wise understanding of our collective consciousness when we connect with others on an emotional level and find a way to work together.

Saturn is in a wide conjunction to his higher octave, Varuna, with both in Cancer. Varuna rules without the need to control or repress and talks about the sovereignty we claim when we dare to be ourselves. This conjunction tells us that Makemake's action will be rigorous and demanding, and the Cancer placement suggests we can nurture an understanding of ourselves through things like routine and commitment, and by being authentic.

This Saturn-Varuna conjunction is at the tip of a cardinal sign T-square. The base of this T-square is an opposition between the Sun-Venus conjunction in Aries, and a Jupiter-Haumea conjunction in Libra. This opposition challenges us to cultivate expansive renewal in our values-driven mission.

The close Sun-Venus conjunction is also conjunct Mercury within 4 degrees, bringing Makemake's inner octave into our

Name: Makemake Discovery
Date: Th., 31 March 2005
Palomar Mountain (P O), CA (US)
116w53, 33n19

Time: 12:00 p.m. hyp.
Univ.Time: 20:00

ASTRO)DIENST
www.astro.com
Type: 2.GW 0.0-1 29-Sep-2023

Event Chart (Method: Web Style / Placidus)
Sun sign: Aries

		C	F	M
F		☉ ☿ ♀ ♋ Er	Or	☽ ♇ Ix Qu
A		♃ ♅ Ha	♂ ⚷ ♊ Go	
E				Se	Ma
W		♄ Va	?	♆ Sa

Sun	11 Ari 11'48"
Moon	25 Sag 26'19"
Mercury	7 Ari 14'27"r
Venus	11 Ari 22'18"
Mars	8 Aqu 0'57"
Jupiter	14 Lib 19'56"r
Saturn	20 Can 28'52"
Uranus	8 Pis 30'41"
Neptune	16 Aqu 57'32"
Pluto	24 Sag 30'32"r
True Node	22 Ari 48'30"d
Desc.T.Node	22 Lib 48'30"d
Chiron	2 Aqu 24' 9"
Ceres	24 Sco 43'16"r
136 Haumea	11 Lib 29'55"r
2 Makemake	20 Vir 15'37"r
48 Gonggong	29 Aqu 57'25"
147 Salacia	15 Pis 38' 2"
199 Eris	20 Ari 18'22"
78 Ixion	11 Sag 1'10"r
82 Orcus	25 Leo 10'39"r
50 Quaoar	15 Sag 3'10"r
77 Sedna	18 Tau 22'44"
20 Varuna	13 Can 45'27"

values-driven mission. Mercury's detailed organizational ability helps us to integrate and disseminate our bird's-eye view. Mercury is semisextile his higher octave Uranus, in Pisces, which gives us an intuitive spiritual understanding of our detailed big picture.

Mercury is sextile, and Uranus is semisextile, Mars in Aquarius. This jump-steps our ideas through intuitive understanding into action in the collective consciousness. Mars is conjunct Chiron which reinforces the Moon-Pluto transformation process of our growth, as we engage higher consciousness understanding.

Challenging aspects from Ceres and Haumea to the grand fire trine and the cardinal T-square suggest that Makemake's big picture will motivate us to integrate a greater awareness of food supplies, cycles of existence, and how we reciprocally nourish ourselves and our world into his values-driven expression in our lives.

Astrological Meaning

Makemake is a spiritual trickster who allows us to experiment with the area of life signified by his position in our chart. He drives spirit into our lives and opens us to the new richness of sacred consciousness. When we are in tune with this sacred consciousness, we understand that we are each a speck in the vast universe, and yet the spirit energies can flow into us and nourish us when we are devoted and in the natural rhythm.

He encourages us to see ourselves as an organic whole. We are not just the sum of our disparate parts, we are a living being in which the parts work together to bring us to life. And he encourages us to look at our community in the same way and understand the role we are playing in the larger organic wholes that we are part of. The first of these is our family, and then our school, work, and all the other teams of which we are a member.

The members of a team work together. Through participation and understanding the teamwork process, we learn how to be sensitive and tune in to our fellow team members. As we connect to others on an empathic level, we tune into collective consciousness and find a way to work together. When we come to see and understand how we are affected by our social context, we are able to be in the right place at the right time to play our part.

We can look at Makemake as the higher octave of Uranus, which is traditionally the higher octave of Mercury. Makemake gives Uranus's intuitive impulses meaning and context, which transforms our understanding of his unexpected ways. And Uranus's lateral web gives Mercury's detail an energetic network to organize and connect his information.

Makemake is keen to learn, he shares Mercury's curiosity, but he is looking at the bigger picture as well as the detail. He talks about freedom, expansiveness, and keen vision, and he encourages us to develop a richer awareness by taking old ideas and playing with them experimentally to liberate the active components.

We know that Uranus brings us intuitive insights, and we have to honor them for the valuable insights that they are, and act on them, or we risk whatever it is manifesting in our lives in a more Saturnian way, so that we eventually get the lesson. With Makemake we need to embrace the rich culture that is created through all these insights. There is an inherent fractal structure in the rich detail of our lives, so that any part of the structure references all other parts.

Makemake reveals this structure, which is the model that we build of our world from Uranus's intuitive flashes. There is no real world, there are just phenomena which we interpret based on our experience. We then react, based on that interpretation, and so shape our reality through those responses.

So we create our world by how we perceive it and interact with it. Until now, this has largely been an unconscious process, but as we embrace this new energy, we begin to understand the creative power of our personal view of reality. This is the power that 'great minds' have to shape the consensus view.

However, when we are at inner planet consciousness, we likely have a more limited, short-term view, which encourages us to cut corners where we see that we can. At this level, Makemake can encourage us to be reckless, and our irreverence of traditional ideas can lead us to engage in double talk and be manipulative with our communication.

We might lose sight of the bigger picture and, as a result, we may not want to play by the rules or cooperate with others. We could indulge in practices such as backbiting and rivalry, which undermine our own position. Or we could try to hog the limelight, rather than humbly play our part, sabotaging the collective success.

We could also take flight to avoid the consequences of our actions or develop an ability to hide in plain sight as a coping skill. Makemake gives us the understanding of the context of each moment and, at this level, we may use that understanding to blend into the background. We become like one of those characters in television ads who are wearing clothes that are patterned like the wallpaper, so we are only seen when we move.

As we develop a more spiritual approach, however, we can find the devotional focus to understand the rich tapestry of our lives that each moment holds. This contact with the bountifulness of cosmic consciousness allows us to joyfully participate in our lives because we feel the profoundness in each experience.

The more we develop spiritually, the more Makemake's cosmic consciousness cuts through our personal feelings to reveal the bigger perspective that we need in order to transform our understanding of ourselves. We then learn to work together and honor our relationships with what we call our 'resources'.

At this level, we are able to alchemically break down existing ideas into their component parts and put them back together in new configurations. We understand the context behind the ideas, and this enables us to be playful in this process. As we formulate our new ideas, we become inspired to put them into reality by winnowing them down into usable applications.

And at the spiritually evolved level, we can see the big picture and integrate this with our personal devotional focus at such a deep level that it will likely be called genius. As we deepen this understanding, we experience the world as an organic whole, which allows us to participate as fully as possible.

At this level we know that we'll get best results when we embrace our dharma with an unflinching gaze and fierce grace that leaves no detail out. Everything that we discover becomes a valuable, creative resource for our growth. We are able to see things as they are and have the power to take action in the face of any eventuality.

Embracing the New Richness

We need to embrace the rich culture that is created through our insights. And we have to trust in our reality model and use it to engage with the world, rather than use it as a camouflage to keep us safe from attention. It works both ways: the more we can engage with the world, the more opportunity we have to refine our model and develop it.

We have to get in our model and drive it around, in order to continually update it based on our new experiences. The more we expand and test our dataset, the better our model becomes and the more useful it is in charting our way forward. Playfulness is a way of removing the fear of failure in this process. There is no failure because all the data is valuable. It's only a failure if we don't integrate the experience, so that the 'bad' outcome happens again.

The challenge with this is that our reality model is not a toy car we can play with. We are cultivating an ineffable, infinitely complex understanding which unconsciously informs our choices in each moment. So, the way we get in it and drive it around is to simply face up to the challenges we encounter each day.

Our reality model is reinforced by the patterns in our lives. If we feel constrained or uninspired by our model, we can try putting ourselves in a new situation to see how our understanding develops in that context. And remember that a playful attitude is the best way to approach this new divine consciousness.

Case Study - Ada Lovelace

Case studies enable us to see how Makemake manifests in someone's life, and thereby understand the action of the planet. Ada Lovelace was the only legitimate child of the renowned poet, Lord Byron. He separated from Ada's mother a month after her birth, left England permanently, and died when she was eight.

She had Makemake conjunct her MC, which is our place in society. Any planet conjunct the MC shapes the role we play, so her cosmic understanding was destined to play a formative role in shaping society. She is chiefly known for her work with Charles Babbage on the design of the Analytical Engine, which was the first computer. The machine was never made, but she wrote the description of how it would work. And today we call this description an algorithm, so she was essentially the first computer programmer.

She was good at maths from an early age and was determined to be a mathematician. She later said, *"That brain of mine is something more than merely mortal; as time will show."*

Makemake was closely square her Moon in the 12th which was closely conjunct her Ascendent. Her mother gave her a good education but dominated and controlled her, which caused her to be socially repressed. With few friends, she married an older man at 19 and had three children before she was 24.

Time: 1:00 p.m. LMT
Univ.Time: 13:00:40
Sid. Time: 18:13:32

ASTRO DIENST
www.astro.com

Type: 2.GW 0.0-1 29-Sep-2023

Natal Chart (Method: Web Style / Placidus)
Sun sign: Sagittarius
Ascendant: Aries

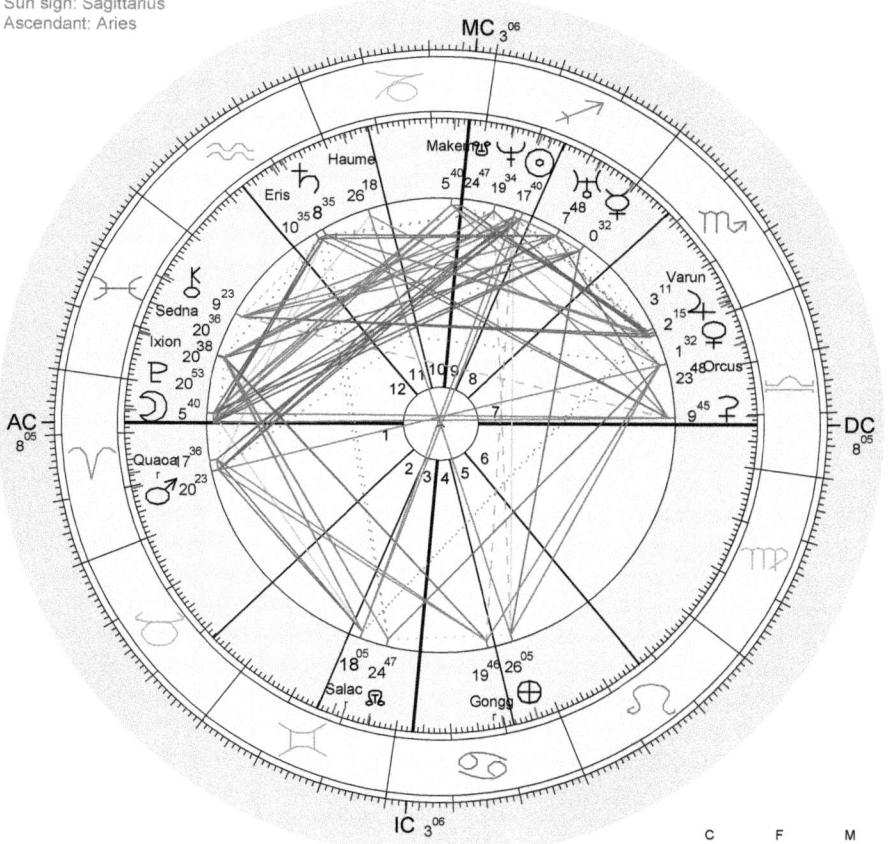

		C	F	M
F		☽ ♂ QuAC		☉ ☿ ♃ ♅ ♆
A		♀ Or	♄ Er	♌ Sa
E		HaMaMC		
W		⊕ Go	♀ ♃ Va	♇ ⚷ Ix Se

☉ Sun	17 Sag 40'17"	
☽ Moon	5 Ari 36'32"	
☿ Mercury	0 Sag 31'54"	
♀ Venus	1 Sco 32'21"	
♂ Mars	20 Ari 23'17"	
♃ Jupiter	2 Sco 14'40"	
♄ Saturn	8 Aqu 34'41"	
♅ Uranus	7 Sag 48' 1"	
♆ Neptune	19 Sag 44'18"	
♇ Pluto	20 Pis 53' 8"	
⚻ True Node	24 Gem 46'47"	
⚼ Desc.T.Node	24 Sag 46'47"	
⚷ Chiron	9 Pis 23'20"	
⊕ P.Fort.	26 Can 4'45"	
⚳ Ceres	9 Lib 44'48"	
136108 Haumea	26 Cap 17'57"	
225088 Gonggong	19 Can 46'29"r	
120347 Salacia	18 Gem 5'25"r	
136199 Eris	10 Aqu 36'13"	
28978 Ixion	20 Pis 37'53"	
90482 Orcus	23 Lib 48' 1"	
50000 Quaoar	17 Ari 35'58"r	
90377 Sedna	23 Pis 36' 2"	
20000 Varuna	20 Sco 10'32"	

AC: 8 Ari 5'29"	2: 22 Tau 13'	3: 15 Gem 12'	
MC: 3 Cap 6'16"	11: 21 Cap 37'	12: 17 Aqu 7'	

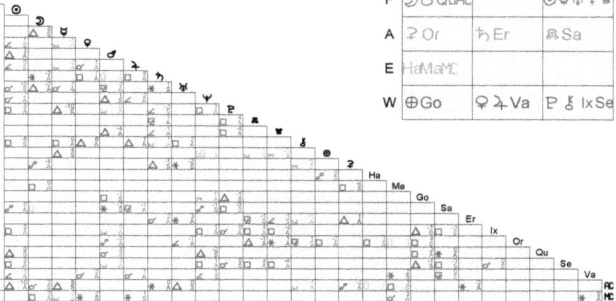

Her Makemake however, was quintile her Orcus and sextile her 7th house stellium of Varuna, Jupiter & Venus. She met Professor Babbage at a party when she was 18. They became friends and 9 years later she became his assistant.

Orcus in the 7th gave her a tenacity and resourcefulness in her one-to-one contacts, and the quintile with Makemake brought evolutionary opportunities to transmute shadow into light through these contacts. In this case, transmuting ignorance into knowledge through her work with Babbage. And the sextile to her Varuna, Jupiter and Venus conjunction, also in the 7th, meant that she would become famous through this relationship. Varuna encourages us to claim our sovereignty and as we do this, we gain an authentic notoriety.

Transit Case Study – Meeting Charles Babbage

Our transiting planets show how the various aspects of our personality and consciousness are manifesting in, and developing through, the events in our lives. We know her meeting with Babbage was formative in her development and, fortunately, we have the date of the party, which was 5 June 1833. So, let's look at her transits on that day.

Mercury in the 2nd house was closely biquintile her Makemake, which is an evolutionary flow between her communication and her innate greater understanding. The meeting opened her eyes to the larger view of society which she inherently understood.

Transiting Ixion in her 1st house was trine her natal Makemake within 1 degree. Ixion encourages us to follow our passion and be irreverent to the traditional boundaries. To ask: Are the rules we're playing by the right ones? Then he prods us to try new approaches and ask for forgiveness afterwards, rather than permission before.

Name: ♀ Ada Lovelace [Adb]
born on Su., 10 December 1815
in London, ENG (UK)
0w10, 51n30

Time: 1:00 p.m.
Univ.Time: 13:00:40
Sid. Time: 18:13:32

ASTRO·DIENST
www.astro.com
Type: 2.GW 0.0-1 29-Sep-2023

Natal Chart (Method: Web Style / Placidus)
Sun sign: Sagittarius
Ascendant: Aries
Transits 5 June 1833

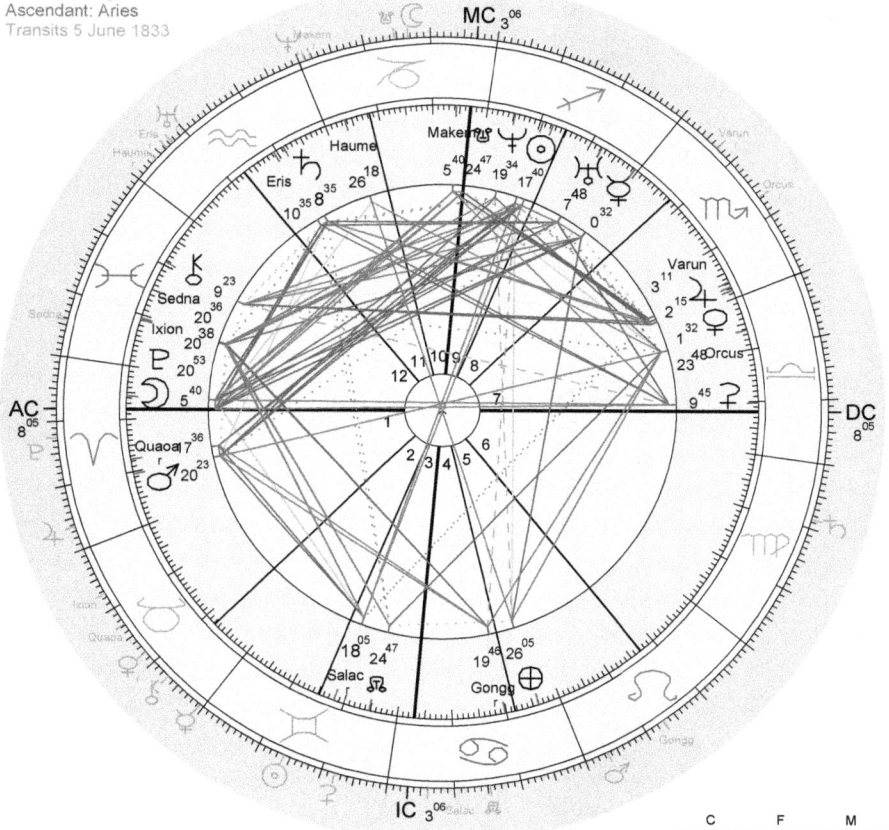

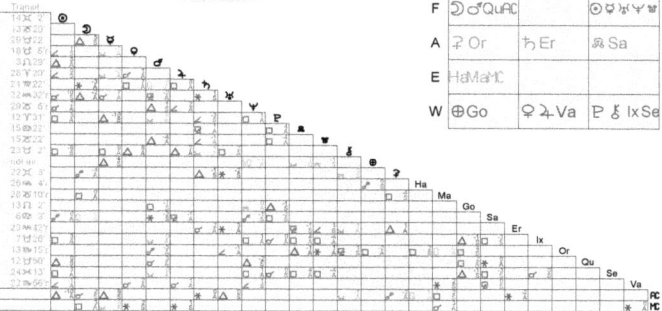

	Natal		Transit
☉ Sun	17 Sag 40'17"		14 ♊ 2'
☽ Moon	8 Ari 39'32"		13 ♒ 30'
☿ Mercury	0 Sag 31'54"		29 ♉ 22'
♀ Venus	1 Sco 32'21"		18 ♋ 57'
♂ Mars	20 Ari 23'17"		3 ♋ 29'
♃ Jupiter	2 Sco 14'40"		28 ♍ 20'
♄ Saturn	8 Aqu 34'41"		21 ♏ 22'
♅ Uranus	7 Sag 48' 1"		32 ♈ 32'r
♆ Neptune	19 Sag 34'18"		29 ♑ 6'r
♇ Pluto	20 Pis 53' 5"		13 ♈ 31'
☊ True Node	24 Gem 46'47"		15 ♑ 22'
☋ Desc.T.Node	24 Sag 46'47"		15 ♋ 22'
⚷ Chiron	9 Pis 23'20"		23 ♉ 2'
⊕ P.Fort.	26 Can 4'45"		10 ♈ 49'
⚳ Ceres	9 Lib 44'48"		22 ♒ 3'
136108 Eris	10 Aqu 35'13"		23 ♈ 57'r
136472 Makemake	5 Cap 39'55"		20 ♊ 10'r
225088 Gonggong	19 Can 46'29"r		13 ♑ 2'
120347 Salacia	18 Gem 5'25"r		6 ♑ 3'
136199 Eris	10 Aqu 35'13"		23 ♈ 57'r
28978 Ixion	20 Pis 37'53"		7 ♉ 50'
90482 Orcus	23 Lib 48' 1"		13 ♑ 15'
50000 Quaoar	17 Ari 35'58"r		12 ♑ 50'
90377 Sedna	20 Pis 36' 2"		24 ♈ 13'
20000 Varuna	3 Sco 10'33"		23 ♋ 56'
AC: 8 Ari 5'29"	2: 22 Tau 13'	3: 15 Gem 12'
MC: 3 Cap 6'16"	11: 21 Cap 37'	12: 17 Aqu 7'

	C	F	M
F	☽ ♂ Qu AC		☉ ♀ ♅ ♆ ♒
A	♃ Or	♄ Er	♏ Sa
E	Ha Ma MC		
W	⊕ Go	♀ ♃ Va	♇ ⚷ Ix Se

41

Nataly, she had a very strong Sedna, Ixion and Pluto conjunction in the 12th house. Sedna rules Artificial Intelligence, so together with devil-may-care Ixion and the powerful, transformative energy of Pluto in the house of the collective unconscious, she was able to change the zeitgeist with her work.

With Ixion transiting in the 1st, she was in a phase of embodying that independent energy in her essence. The trine to her natal Makemake as she met Babbage indicates their relationship was a key opportunity to let herself out to play and develop her big picture understanding.

Meanwhile, transiting Makemake in the 11th house was conjunct her natal Haumea within 1 degree. Haumea is the planet of rebirth and she is in the house of collective consciousness. Obviously there was a rejuvenation in the collective consciousness through Ada's work as the first computer programmer. We see Haumea's long-term action in the fact that this rebirth took a couple of hundred years to manifest. Babbage couldn't find the funds to make his engine, but he and Ada planted the seed that future generations developed.

Transiting Makemake was also sextile her Mercury in the 8th house, within 2 degrees. Mercury in the 8th likes parties and transiting Makemake was opening her mind through their communication as they met.

Finally, transiting Makemake was also opposite her Part of Fortune within 2 degrees in the 5th house of creativity and love and square her Venus within 3 degrees in the 7th house. These transits challenged her to form a one-to-one relationship which was meaningful in a big-picture Makemakian way.

Transit Case Study – Claims Special Talents

In 1841 her letters began to claim special intellectual talents. As we shall see, these are Makemakian talents. On 6 February, she wrote to her mother that she felt herself to be *"pre-eminently a discoverer of the hidden realities of nature;"* this by virtue of her special intellectual talents.

First, owing to what she called *"a peculiarity in her nervous system,"* she claimed to have:

> *"perceptions of some things, which no one else has; or at least very few, if any. This faculty may be designated in me as a singular tact, or some might say an intuitive perception of things hidden from eyes, ears & the ordinary senses."*[6]

Second, she claimed, *"immense reasoning faculties;"* and third, what she called her:

> *"concentrative faculty, by which I mean the power not only of throwing my whole energy & existence into whatever I choose, but also bringing to bear on any one subject or idea, a vast apparatus from all sorts of apparently irrelevant & extraneous sources. I can throw rays from every quarter of the universe into one vast focus."*[7]

It sounds very Makemake, so what were her transits? During this period, she had Makemake transiting through her 11th house of collective consciousness, closely conjunct her Saturn, and sextile her Uranus in the 8th house of collective energies.

---

6   https://psychclassics.yorku.ca/Lovelace/intro.htm
7   https://psychclassics.yorku.ca/Lovelace/intro.htm

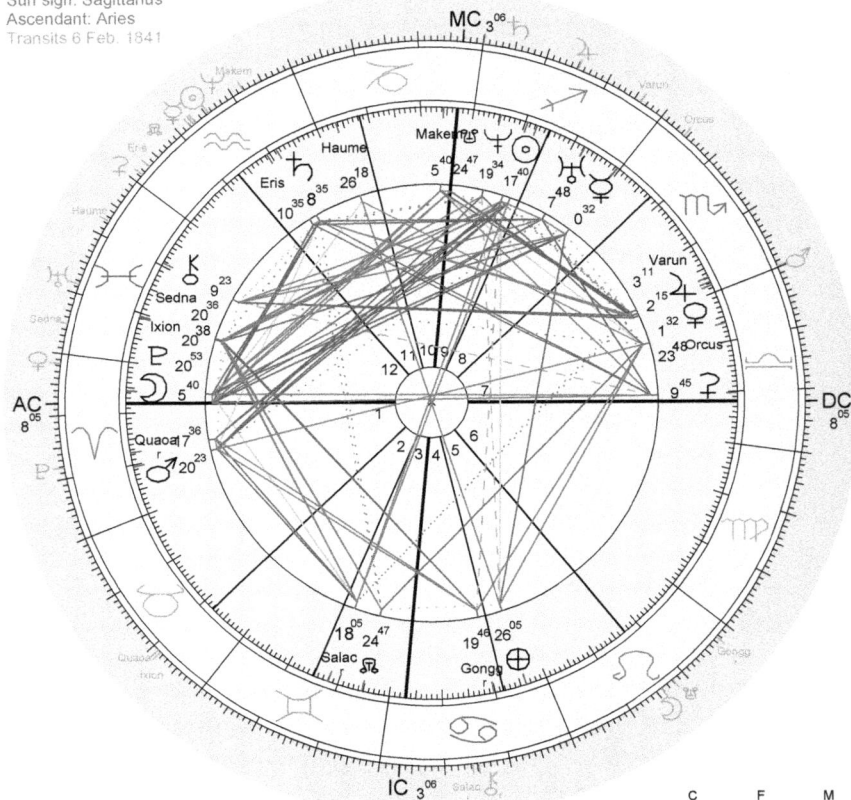
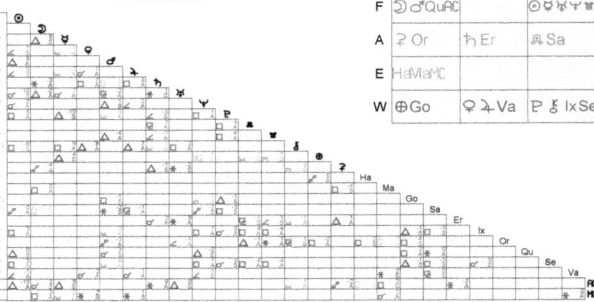

Mirroring this, she had Uranus transiting through her 12th house of the unconscious, quintile her natal Makemake in the 10th house. As we've seen, Makemake is the higher octave of Uranus, so these mirroring transits bring the octaves strongly into alignment.

Quintiles are evolutionary flows where we can integrate the energies at either end at such depth that we take it to a new level of being. And the quintile from transiting Uranus to her natal Makemake was in operation for the whole period that she was claiming special powers. So, the reality is that she did have those powers.

Transit Case Study – Publication of First Computer Program

Finally, let's look at Ada's transits for the publication of her translation of the Italian article: *"Sketch of the Analytical Engine invented by Charles Babbage"*, together with her notes on how it would function. She began work on the translation in February of 1843 and when she presented it to Babbage, he suggested that she write the notes explaining parts that had been left vague in the original.

She worked closely with him on these notes throughout the spring and summer of 1843 and they grew to be twice as long as the article itself. They exchanged dozens of letters and drafts and also met frequently. The notes were completed by August 1843, and they appeared in Volume 3 of Taylor's Scientific Memoirs in September 1843.

At the time of publication, she had transiting Jupiter traveling with transiting Neptune, both in her 12th house and both closely semisquare her Makemake in the 10th. So, her professional understanding generated an expansive inspirational event in the zeitgeist, which was nothing less than the conception of computers.

Meanwhile, transiting Ixion was encouraging her to follow her bliss in the 2nd house of material reality and, when the article was published, he was very closely biquintile her Makemake in the 10th. Her irreverent passion in the material world was in an evolutionary flow with her big-picture social role.

Transiting Varuna, the higher octave of Saturn, in the 8th house, was semisextile within 1 degree, showing that she was claiming her sovereignty in the collective energies through the publication and thereby gaining a degree of immortality through that fame.

And while transiting Uranus in the 12th house was quintile when she was claiming special powers, now it is squaring her Makemake, so she was being challenged to manifest her intuitive understanding in the world through the publication.

Nataly, she had Saturn conjunct Eris within 2 degrees in the 12th house. Transiting Makemake was closely conjunct her Saturn as she was claiming special intellectual talents and closely conjunct Eris as the article was published. Eris brings the full light of consciousness to whatever she touches, so the conjunction of transiting Makemake represents the spirit guidance coming through. She's channelling.

Makemake is also sesquiquadrate her North Node in the 3rd house, challenging her to fulfil her destiny with her ideas and communication, which she was doing through the publication.

"I never am really satisfied that I understand anything; because understand it well as I may, my comprehension can only be an infinitesimal fraction of all I want to understand about the many connections and relations which occur to me, how the matter in question was first thought of or arrived at...".[8]

---

8   https://www.goodreads.com/author/quotes/3950749.Ada_ Lovelace#

Name: ♀ Ada Lovelace [Adb]
born on Su., 10 December 1815
in London, ENG (UK)
0w10, 51n30

Time: 1:00 p.m.
Univ.Time: 13:00:40
Sid. Time: 18:13:32

ASTRO)DIENST
www.astro.com

Type: 2.GW 0.0-1 29-Sep-2023

Natal Chart (Method: Web Style / Placidus)
Sun sign: Sagittarius
Ascendant: Aries
Transits 1 Sept. 1843

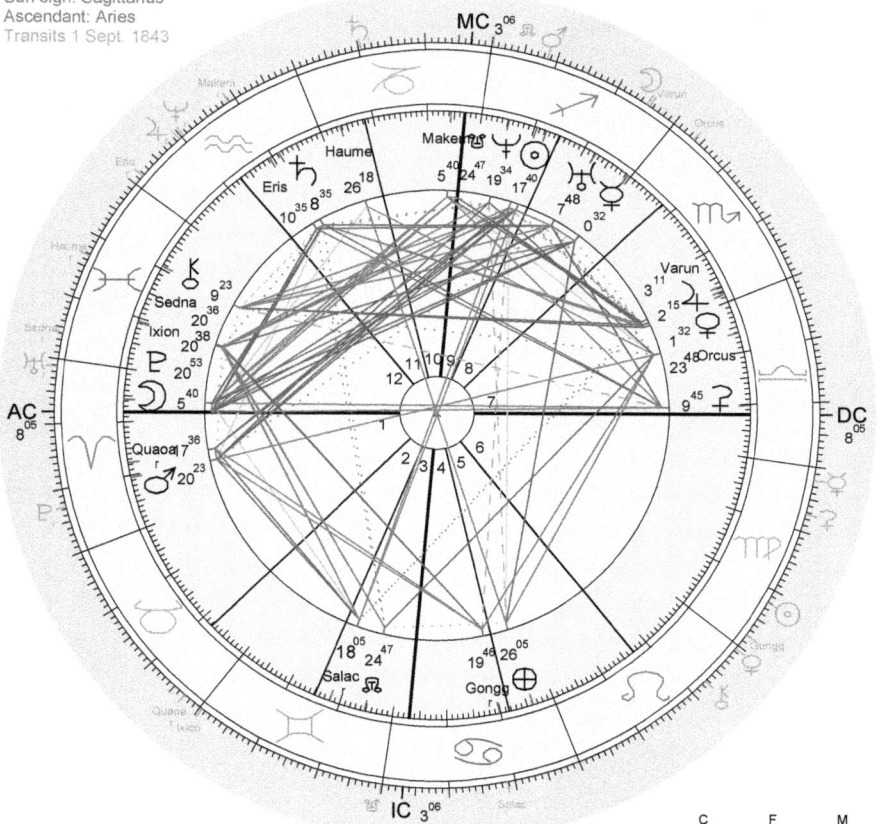

	Natal	Travel
⊙ Sun	17 Sag 40'17"	7 Sag 55'3"
☽ Moon	5 Ari 39'32"	5 Vir 0"
☿ Mercury	0 Sag 31'54"	22 Vir 59"
♀ Venus	1 Sco 32'21"	26 Lib 33"
♂ Mars	20 Ari 23'17"	21 Vir 26"
♃ Jupiter	2 Sco 14'40"	20 Aqu 32"
♄ Saturn	8 Aqu 34'41"	25 Aqu 53"
♅ Uranus	7 Sag 48' 1"	1 Ari 11"
♆ Neptune	19 Sag 34'18"	18 Aqu 36"
♇ Pluto	20 Pis 53' 5"	22 Ari 43"
⚷ True Node	24 Gem 46'47"	20 Ari 47"
☋ Desc.T.Node	24 Sag 46'47"	20 Lib 47"
⚷ Chiron	9 Pis 23'20"	22 Pis 40"
⊗ P.Fort.	26 Can 4'46"	24 Aqu 25"
⚳ Ceres	9 Lib 44'48"	22 Vir 41"
136108 Haumea	26 Cap 17'57"	11 Vir 55"
136472 Makemake	5 Cap 39'55"	11 Vir 63"
225088 Gonggong	19 Can 46'29"r	2 Vir 4"
120347 Salacia	18 Gem 5'25"r	16 Vir 49"
136199 Eris	10 Aqu 35'13"	26 Aqu 57"
28978 Ixion	20 Pis 37'63"	0 Ari 34"
90482 Orcus	23 Lib 46' 1"	26 Vir 10"
50000 Quaoar	17 Ari 35'58"r	4 Vir 58"
90377 Sedna	20 Pis 36' 2"	25 Ari 49"r
20000 Varuna	3 Sco 10'32"	4 Vir 28"
AC: 8 Ari 5'28"	**2:** 22 Tau 13'	**3:** 15 Gem 12'
MC: 3 Cap 8'16"	**11:** 21 Cap 30'	**12:** 17 Aqu 7'

	C	F	M
F	☽ ♂ QuAC		⊙ ☿ ♄ ♅ ♆ ♇
A	♃ Or	♄ Er	♏ Sa
E	HaMaMC		
W	⊕ Go	♀ ♃ Va	♇ ⚷ IxSe

47

Case Study – David Shiner

David Shiner is an American actor, clown, physical comedian, playwright, and director. He has Makemake closely conjunct his Ascendent and closely sextile his Mercury in the 3rd house, so he exemplifies the trickster side of Makemake.

Usually donning a small dunce cap, he started as a street mime, first in Colorado, and later in France and Germany. He drew hundreds of spectators at a time to his own form of guerrilla theater, in which he incorporated audience members and bystanders as actors in a drama. He described this work as *"holding up a mirror to both the mundane and spectacular as an antagonistic yet lovable social commentator"*[9].

His Makemake is also closely semisextile his Ceres-Haumea conjunction in the 2nd house, which enabled him to birth this new theatre form. Makemake is also semisextile his Jupiter on the cusp of his 12th house, so he can connect with the collective unconscious in the audience.

In the early 1990's he was featured in Cirque du Soleil's production *Nouvelle Expérience*, and because of his antics, which included stepping through, on and over much of the crowd and the staging of a mock silent-movie melodrama with four members of the audience, he may be the best remembered of the Cirque's clowns.

"You have to like people a lot. When I bring someone on stage, I want to make sure they have fun. I'm not there to make them

---

9   https://www.david-shiner.com/david-shiner

Name: ♂ David Shiner [Adb]
born on Su., 13 September 1953
in Boston MA, USA
71w03, 42n21

Time: 1:50 a.m.
Univ.Time: 5:50
Sid. Time: 0:33:31

ASTRO·DIENST
www.astro.com
Type: 2.GW 0.0-1 29-Sep-2023

Natal Chart (Method: Web Style / Placidus)
Sun sign: Virgo
Ascendant: Cancer

☉ Sun	20 Vir	8'43"
☽ Moon	13 Sco	53' 8"
☿ Mercury	25 Vir	16'32"
♀ Venus	16 Leo	50'40"
♂ Mars	29 Leo	2'50"
♃ Jupiter	24 Gem	51' 2"
♄ Saturn	26 Lib	25'45"
♅ Uranus	22 Can	10'20"
♆ Neptune	22 Lib	24'23"
♇ Pluto	23 Leo	47'23"
☊ True Node	2 Aqu	0'11"
☋ Desc.T.Node	2 Leo	0'11"
⚷ Chiron	18 Cap	22'21"r
⊕ P.Fort.	2 Gem	54'15"
⚵ Ceres	26 Leo	30'26"
136108 Haumea	24 Leo	46'51"
136472 Makemake	28 Can	14'40"
225088 Gonggong	8 Aqu	20'14"r
120347 Salacia	4 Cap	2'36"r
136199 Eris	8 Ari	9' 5"r
90482 Orcus	1 Can	2' 4"
28978 Ixion	17 Lib	43'57"
50000 Quaoar	10 Lib	12' 9"
90377 Sedna	26 Ari	4'45"r
20000 Varuna	7 Tau	59'18"r

AC: 26 Can 38'40" 2: 16 Leo 3' 3: 9 Vir 17'
MC: 9 Ari 7'14" 11: 16 Tau 8' 12: 24 Gem 19'

	C	F	M
F	ErSeMC	♀♂♇♃Ha	
A	♄♆IxQu♫Go		♃⊕
E	⚷Sa	Va	☉☿
W	♃(MaOr♈☽		

49

look stupid—although I do that! But they end up having fun watching me make fun of them."[10]

His Makemake is also closely square both his Saturn in the 4th house and his Sedna in the 10th house. Sedna in the 10th brings transcendent learning experiences in society, where we are forced to let go of our old framework of consciousness and transcend to a new, more spiritual, perspective. And the opposition between Sedna and Saturn means that these will be real world confrontations.

Transit Case Study – Cirque du Soleil's *Koozå*

Let's see how this played out through his transits. In 2007, he wrote and directed Cirque du Soleil's highly successful production *Koozå*.

Kooza was a return to the origins of Cirque du Soleil, combining the two circus traditions of acrobatics and clowning in spectacular style. Set in an electrifying and exotic visual world full of surprises, thrills and chills, it tells the story of The Innocent, a melancholy loner in search of his place in the world, through contortionists, trapeze-artists, the high wire and the breath-taking 'Wheel of Death'.

The show opened on 19th April, 2007, when transiting Jupiter in his 5th house was in a close evolutionary biquintile with his natal Makemake, bringing luck and success with his creative work.

Transiting Orcus in the 2nd house was closely semisextile his Makemake. Orcus transmutes shadow into light, and the light of laughter is what clown and comedy is all about. This 2nd house transit brought him income from creating that light.

---

10 https://www.broadway.com/buzz/183971/old-hats-stars-david-shiner-bill-irwin-on-clowning-around-together-for-25-years/

Name: ♂ David Shiner [Adb]
born on Su., 13 September 1953
in Boston MA, USA
71w03, 42n21

Time: 1:50 a.m.
Univ.Time: 5:50
Sid. Time: 0:33:31

ASTRO DIENST
www.astro.com
Type: 2.GW 0.0-1 29-Sep-2023

Natal Chart (Method: Web Style / Placidus)
Sun sign: Virgo
Ascendant: Cancer
Transits 19 Apr. 2007

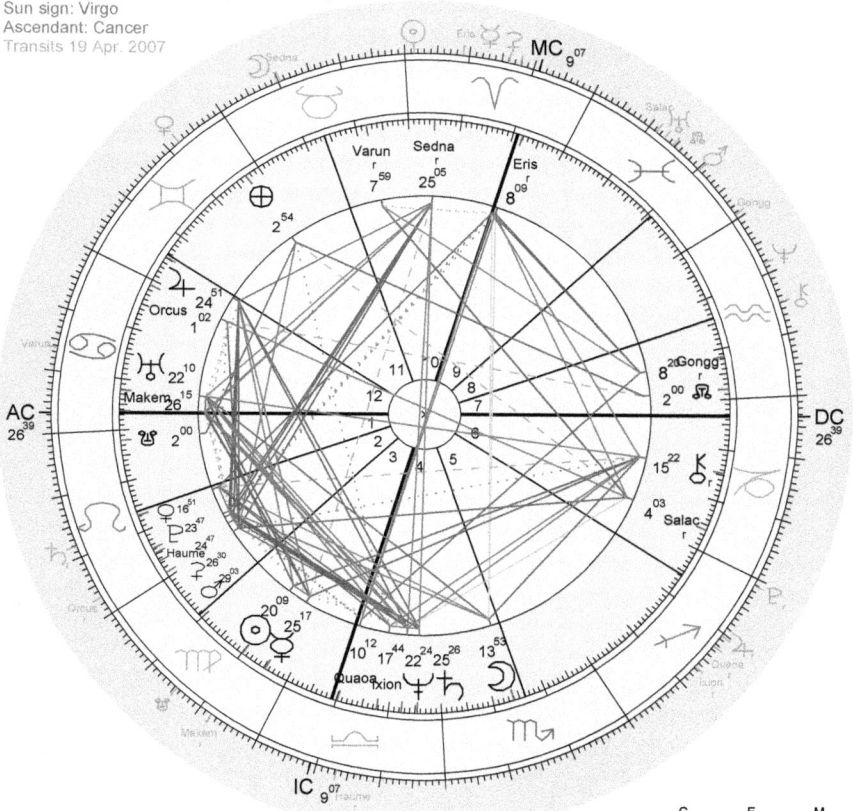

	Natal	Transit
☉ Sun	20 Vir 8'43"	
☽ Moon	13 Sco 53' 8"	
☿ Mercury	25 Vir 18'32"	
♀ Venus	16 Leo 50'40"	
♂ Mars	29 Leo 2'50"	
♃ Jupiter	24 Gem51' 2"	
♄ Saturn	25 Lib 26'45"	
♅ Uranus	22 Can 10'20"	
♆ Neptune	22 Lib 24'23"	
♇ Pluto	23 Leo 47'23"	
☊ True Node	2 Aqu 0'11"	
☋ Desc.T.Node	2 Leo 0'11"	
⚷ Chiron	15 Cap 22'21"r	
⊕ P.Fort.	26 Gem54'15"	
⚵ Ceres	26 Leo 30'26"	
136108 Haumea	24 Leo 46'51"r	
136472 Makemake	26 Can 14'40"	
225088 Gonggong	8 Aqu 20'14"r	
120347 Salacia	4 Cap 2'36"r	
136199 Eris	8 Ari 9' 57"r	
28978 Ixion	17 Lib 43'57"r	
90482 Orcus	1 Can 2' 4"	
50000 Quaoar	10 Lib 12' 9"	
90377 Sedna	25 Ari 4'45"r	
20000 Varuna	7 Tau 59'18"r	
AC: 26 Can 38'46"	2: 16 Leo	3: 9 Vir 31'
MC: 9 Ari 7'14"	11:16 Tau	12: 24 Gem19'

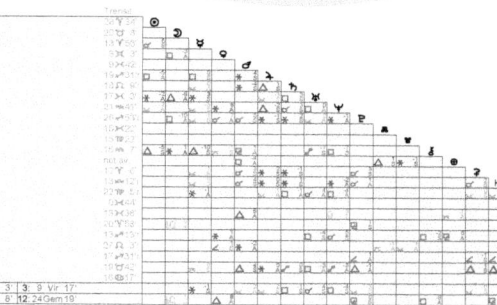

	C	F	M
F	ErSeMC	♀♂♇♅♃Ha	
A	♄♆IxQu♏Go		♃⊕
E	⚷Sa	Va	☉☿
W	♅(MaOrAC☽		

51

Makemake was transiting his 3rd house, closely sextile his Uranus in the 12th house. So, his big picture understanding in the house of ideas and communication was flowing with his ability to tune in to the collective unconscious.

Transiting Makemake was also closely semisextile his Neptune in the 4th house, flowing with his visionary approach in his sacred space. And it was also tightly sesquiquadrate his Varuna in the 10th house, challenging him to claim his sovereignty as a playwright and director. Which he did, as this has become one of Cirque du Soleil's most successful shows.

Makemake had been transiting over his Sun in the 3rd house for the past couple of years, as the show came together, and it was still conjunct his Sun, within 1 degree, and approaching a conjunction with his Mercury, within 3 degrees, at the Kooza premiere. Through this period his big picture understanding was merging with his will and ability to communicate.

And finally, transiting Makemake was square his Jupiter on the 12th house cusp within 2 degrees. The squares are structural, they are defining, so this was an important moment in his growth to becoming the big-picture person that his Makemake enables. If he hadn't refined his understanding of people and society sufficiently, this square would ensure the launch was a flop to create a crisis of understanding. Since he has refined his understanding, the square becomes a support, signaling the success of the production.

Transit Case Study – Cirque du Soleil's *Banana Shpeel*

Following *Kooza*, Shiner then wrote and directed Cirque's infamous *Banana Shpeel* which was one of the most unsuccessful shows the company has produced. It premiered two years later, in 2009, and was cancelled soon the following year due to the poor reception by audiences and critics alike.

This was the first and only time Cirque du Soleil has cancelled a show.

Let's look at David's transits on the opening night, which was in New York on the 21st May, 2010. That day both transiting Gonggong in the 8th house of collective energies, and transiting Quaoar in the 5th house of creativity, were biquintile his natal Makemake.

So, we've got this show which is not going to be successful, or will not be well received, and there are two potentially positive evolutionary flows to his Makemake as it premieres. How shall we understand this? The biquintiles take the energies at either end to a new level, but how they operate with these outer planets depends on our current consciousness. And in order to enable the aspect we have to actively engage with the planets and do the work they require.

Transiting Quaoar in the 5th house of creativity is encouraging him to do a "new" show, something that they haven't done before, but the name *Banana Shpeel* suggests it's actually traditional comedy. Shpeel means "oft-repeated thoughtless dialogue which is not necessarily true", so, if nothing else, it's not a great sales term. So, he's trying to do something new, and he can see that it can work, because of the biquintile, but it's not connecting with the audience.

> *(Cirque CEO) Mr. Lamarre said Cirque wanted to avoid putting labels like "Broadway" and "musical theater" on "Banana Shpeel," so as not to predetermine the shape of the show or the expectations of audience members. Still, he added, "When you're working on a show that you're hoping will be different from other productions out there, you can run into problems as people try to*

determine what the show is."[11]

The other biquintile is from transiting Gonggong in the 8th house, and it may be that he's not really empathizing with the audience. With Gonggong it is important to lift our energy out of our own space, so we can empathize with others. And this is what Shiner was famous for in his work: his empathy. He has Gonggong in his 7th house of one-to-one relationships natally and, as a way of tuning into people, he used to clamber over the backs of the audience seats on his way to the stage to start his show. But the biquintiles are rarefied, so while he created something new, it wasn't something people could relate to.

> *Paul Binder, the founding artistic director of Big Apple Circus, with which Cirque has been competing in New York City in recent years, was invited to a dress rehearsal of "Banana Shpeel" and also attended opening night. While he said he admired much of the talent in the show, he added that he sensed right away that Cirque might have a problem building an audience.*

> *"The reality is, people have very specific expectations with Cirque shows, and 'Banana Shpeel' turned out to be neither fish nor fowl, neither circus act nor theatrical vaudeville entertainment," Mr. Binder said. "So I think it was probably difficult to get a large audience excited about a show when many didn't really understand what it was."[12]*

Transiting Jupiter in the 9th house was trine Shiner's natal Makemake on the opening night and Saturn in the 3rd house was sextile, so the flows to the main structural planets suggest

---

11 https://www.nytimes.com/2010/06/26/theater/26shpeel.html
12 Ibid

Name: ♂ David Shiner [Adb]
born on Su., 13 September 1953
in Boston MA, USA
71w03, 42n21

Time: 1:50 a.m.
Univ.Time: 5:50
Sid. Time: 0:33:31

ASTRO·DIENST
www.astro.com
Type: 2.GW 0.0-1 29-Sep-2023

Natal Chart (Method: Web Style / Placidus)
Sun sign: Virgo
Ascendant: Cancer
Transits 21 May 2010

		Natal	Transit
☉	Sun	20 Vir 8'43"	29 ♉ 51'r
☽	Moon	13 Sco 53' 8"	0 ♈ 1'
☿	Mercury	25 Vir 16'32"	5 ♊ 44'
♀	Venus	16 Leo 50'40"	18 ♋ 6'
♂	Mars	29 Leo 2'50"	21 ♌ 22'
♃	Jupiter	24 Gem 51' 2"	27 ♓ 30'
♄	Saturn	25 Lib 25'45"	27 ♍ 55'r
♅	Uranus	22 Can 10'20"	29 ♓ 40'
♆	Neptune	18 Lib 24'23"	28 ♒ 40'
♇	Pluto	23 Leo 47'23"	4 ♑ 57'r
☊	True Node	2 Aqu 0'11"	12 ♓ 47'
☋	Desc.T.Node	2 Leo 0'11"	12 ♍ 47'
⚷	Chiron	15 Cap 22'21"r	0 ♓ 53'
⊕	P.Fort.	2 Gem 54'15"	not av.
⚳	Ceres	26 Leo 30'26"	3 ♌ 16'
136108 Haumea	24 Can 46'51"	13 ♏ 45'r
136472 Makemake	26 Can 14'40"	24 ♍ 50'r
225088 Gonggong	8 Aqu 20'14"r	1 ♓ 49'
120347 Salacia	4 Cap 2'38"r	23 ♓ 4' 2'
136199 Eris	8 Ari 9' 5"r	21 ♈ 59'
28978 Ixion	17 Lib 43'57"r	16 ♒ 53'
90482 Orcus	1 Can 2' 4"	39 ♌ 50'
50000 Quaoar	10 Lib 12' 9"	20 ♒ 49'r
90377 Sedna	25 Ari 4'45"r	21 ♉ 49'
20000 Varuna	7 Tau 59'18"r	20 ♑ 17'

AC: 26 Can 38'40" 2: 16 Leo 3': 9 Vir 17'
MC: 9 Ari 7'14" 11: 16 Tau 6': 24 Gem 19'

	C	F	M
F	Er SeMC	♀ ♂ ♅ ♇ ♃ Ha	
A	♄ ♆ Ix Qu ☋ Go		♃ ⊕
E	⚷ Sa	Va	☉ ☿
W	♅ ⟨ Ma Or AC ☽		

it should work. Well, the new show is evidence of the Saturn sextile. And people are coming, that's the Jupiter trine.

But we also have transiting Eris in the 10th house squaring his Makemake, within 4 degrees. And that aspect is approaching, so this is the start of a phase in which he is being challenged to take off the blinders. Makemake can give us a devotional perspective which approaches genius, but that can be too narrowly focused.

As a result, he's challenging everyone to see something bigger, and they don't want to. Most people don't go to Cirque du Soleil to be enlightened. Why did it go wrong? He's lost the empathy with the audience and is instead trying to entertain and tell a story in a new avant-garde form that people couldn't relate to.

When *Banana Shpeel* premiered, transiting Makemake in the 3rd house was very closely conjunct his Mercury. The big picture was shining through his communication skills. Makemake is the higher octave of Uranus, which is the higher octave of Mercury. And the higher octaves act on the lower octaves to repolarize them. So Makemake was acting on his Mercury during this transit and repolarizing it into something more spiritual.

Transiting Makemake was also closely squaring Jupiter on the cusp of his 12th house, which was in an approaching two-degree orb when he had success with *Kooza*. The close square means his rich contextual understanding challenged his ability to have success connecting with the collective unconscious. With Makemake we sometimes see a tendency to be too inward-looking, or too specialized, to be able to connect with the broad public.

Transiting Makemake was also inconjunct his Sedna in the 10th house, so it was a really important step in his spiritual destiny that the show didn't work. There is no right and wrong for Sedna. The inconjunct is a push, pull, it's a fated aspect, so it was vital for him to have that 'failure' as far as his soul was concerned.

Transiting Makemake was semi-sextile Pluto in the 2nd house, within 1 degree. Pluto in the 2nd house can be very resourceful, but he also brings the need for that resourcefulness through material instability.

And, finally, transiting Makemake was biquintile his Gonggong in the 7th house, within 1 degree, echoing the biquintile from transiting Gonggong to his natal Makemake. He's getting messages about the use of his empathic abilities in his relationships, and you'd think with the two biquintiles it would work well.

From our research it appears that the vision for the show morphed from a scripted mix of vaudeville, musical theatre, and circus, into a self-devised, vaudeville-inspired clown-ensemble performance. Self-devising is an improvisational process, and he worked hard to re-work the material with the performers on the workshop floor as the New York premier approached. This work is the two biquintiles, working at an evolutionary level with his team to create the rich canvas of the performance.

Both planets are about teamwork and participation at the top level. However, Makemake can be inward-looking and Gonggong can be self-involved. Had this workshopping occurred in front of an audience or, like his early work, in the street, where the responses of the crowd could inform their work, the audience reception of the show would undoubtedly have been better.

Instead, they created a good work of art, which however was not saleable as an entertainment. In the earlier quote from the director of the Big Apple Circus, he was careful to say that he liked the art, but that it didn't have a natural audience because it was new.

Makemake in the Signs

Makemake in Cancer

Makemake ingressed into Cancer in 1930. Those of us with Makemake in Cancer have a sense that the world is an interconnecting organic whole. However, we can also feel that parts of this system are out of balance and, as a generation, we are learning how to embody a system of care.

Makemake's tendency to self-involvement and hiding in plain sight as a coping skill is accentuated here, particularly when we are overwhelmed or feel that we've been taken advantage of. At these times we can happily live in our own world while still in plain sight, and the challenge is to engage our world with a wider context.

We may have a fussy or worried approach to understanding our world, feeling insecure when our view is challenged, or when it proves inadequate. However, as we develop our understanding of ourselves and our world, we learn to make shrewd decisions.

In this sign Makemake understands the organic interplay within any enterprise, and with this placement our ability to act as an organic whole and in a social context is heightened. We understand the nourishment required to sustain each piece of the rich culture we find around us and can tend to it appropriately.

We are pioneering environmental awareness in the world because we understand and champion the inherent interconnection which supports our lives. At higher levels, we are creating contexts within which unconditional love, nurturing, and empowerment have room to take form and play.

Makemake in Leo

Makemake ingressed into Leo in 1957. With this placement we understand the creative potential of each piece of the rich drama in which we find ourselves playing a role. This understanding gives us a way to influence the drama from the inside by playing our part.

Play is important in our exploration of ourselves and our world, and we need the space to be playful with our worldview, in order to develop it. We learn the most when we can allow a trial-and-error process in our lives.

If we are creative, we will put a devotional focus into our creative expression and produce rich textured art in whatever medium we choose. We understand the fractal nature of art and life, where one piece can express both the inclusivity and the diversity of the whole.

With Makemake in Leo, we take pride in the complexity of our understanding and our ability to winnow back to essential applications that benefit all beings. However, we have to be careful not to take an arrogant approach when our understanding is challenged and be judgmental as a result.

We are learning to interface our personal story with the collective story to reach a new synthesis. At the highest level, as we learn to be generous with our understanding, we gain the confidence to take a leading role in both our own and the collective drama.

Makemake in Virgo

Makemake ingressed into Virgo in 1985. With this placement we have a natural intelligence, borne of our experience. Understanding is an alchemical process for us, where we are processing our experience in real time as we turn it into knowledge.

We have a practical understanding of the context of each moment, so we are in touch with the material demands of reality. This means we can work effectively with the building blocks that are available to us.

However, we may tend to be pedantic about our understanding of some topic or be nit-picky about another's understanding. We have to be careful to give ourselves and others room to play and make mistakes, so we can learn.

Those of us with this placement will be attracted to health-based practices which give us a holistic, embodied understanding of ourselves. We could be into physical practices such as aerobics, yoga, or martial arts, which lift our spirit.

At the highest level, when our worldview is informed by spirit, we can be adaptable and productive, because we understand the dynamics behind any of our interactions. We understand what levers we can pull to make changes. We might also be able to find best practice across species to understand how humanity can evolve.

Makemake in Libra

Makemake ingressed into Libra in late 2013. Those of us born with this placement enjoy sharing our personal journey and hearing the stories of others. We are natural communicators and can be very diplomatic because we understand the backstory of what is happening around us.

We want our interactions and the social context around us to be just and fair and, if we find they are not and we are not able to make them so, we might choose to hide in plain sight by blending into the background.

We understand the value of complexity and the importance of context. And with this placement we may sit on the fence, endlessly second-guessing our own understanding, which leads to indecisiveness and lost opportunities. We need to learn to trust in our understanding of whatever is going down, so we can take the initiative with our ideas.

At the same time, we also have to be careful of being judgmental in this understanding because fixed attitudes leave no room for the experimentation and play required in the learning process.

When we give ourselves this freedom, we understand our interactions on an organic level, seeing them as part of a greater whole. And at the highest level, we are able to cultivate collective teamwork that transcends borders as we recognize we're all on the same planet together.

Makemake in the Houses

We see the ethereal energies of the outer planets manifesting most clearly in our personal lives through their house position. The houses represent areas of our lives and they focus a planet's energy and give it a playground.

First House

With Makemake in the 1st House of self, we will be clever and quick-witted and have the devotional focus to understand the rich tapestry that each moment holds. This is also the house of 'how others see us', and with this placement we will likely be thought of as insightful, and act as an inspiration to others.

At the unconscious level however, this is the house of our self-interest and our ego, so when challenged we could respond by being verbally manipulative, or engaging in double talk and diversion of facts, or simply not playing by the rules. This is also the house of our defence mechanisms, and with this placement we could take flight to avoid consequence, or hide as a coping skill.

For example Oliver North was a National Security Council staff member in the USA during the Iran–Contra affair, which was a political scandal involving the illegal sale of weapons to Iran to encourage the release of American hostages then held in Lebanon. North diverted the proceeds from these arms sales to support the Contra rebel groups in Nicaragua. He was convicted of aiding and abetting in the obstruction of Congress, accepting an illegal gratuity, and altering and destroying documents.

When we are on the spiritual path however, we can develop a deep self-awareness. At this level we understand the complexity of groups and cultures and also how they function as an organic whole. We are therefore able to play a facilitating role in these organisations and cultures.

Consider Gertrude Stein, who was an American writer and icon of modernism. She moved to Paris at 29, where she held weekly salons with the likes of Picasso, Hemingway, Wilder, Matisse and F. Scott Fitzgerald in attendance. These gatherings brought together the talent and ideas that would define modern literature and art. Stein described her writing style, not as stream of consciousness, but as an "excess of consciousness".

At the spiritually evolved level we can embody our world view, and we have a vitality and resourcefulness in our joyful participation in our lives. At this level we can find the devotional focus to understand the rich tapestry that each moment holds, and so we can maximize our engagement and impact.

Second House

With Makemake in the 2nd House of resources, we can bring a devotional focus to the process of gaining and spending our money which permits extreme talent in this area, however this can come at the expense of neglecting other things. This is the house of security needs and Makemake can give us fast footwork and an ability to learn from experience, to achieve a comfortable life.

At the unconscious level however, the desire for sensual pleasures might get in the way of the drive for money and possessions, and we could behave recklessly and in a self-serving manner, just looking after ourselves and not playing by the rules or cooperating with others.

However, when we are on the spiritual path we can approach the material world with less attachment and with more of a sense of joyful participation. Through this we build a deeper and more realistic understanding of how it all works. At this level Makemake enriches our values, ensuring we are in the right place at the right time.

Like Marie Curie who, along with her husband, conducted pioneering research on radioactivity, a term she coined. They were awarded the Nobel Prize for Physics when she was 36. She was the first woman to receive a Nobel. She so valued the rich material world that she went on to discover two new elements — polonium and radium — for which she earned a second Nobel Prize, this time for Chemistry.

And at the spiritually evolved level, we learn to value and cultivate both the rich spiritual world and the rich material world around us. At this level Makemake drives spirit into our lives and opens us to see the bigger picture.

Like Richard Tarnas, a US cultural historian, astrologer, and teacher, who did his doctoral dissertation on '*LSD psychotherapy, psychoanalysis, and spiritual rebirth*'. He is well known for his third book *Cosmos and Psyche: Intimations of a New World View*, in which he shows that the major events of Western cultural history correlate consistently and meaningfully with the observed angular positions of the planets.

Third House

With Makemake in the 3rd House of ideas and communication, we will be clever, quick-witted and verbally self-assured. This is the house of our thinking patterns and Makemake, being a spiritual trickster, allows us to experiment with these.

At the unconscious level, however, we might get lost in

the details and the small bits of information, or be verbally manipulative, engaging in double talk and simply not being straight with the facts. At this level we could also be into gossip, or engage in backbiting and rivalry. And we may take flight to avoid the consequences of our actions or develop an ability to hide in plain sight as a coping skill.

When we are on the spiritual path, however, we learn to make the right connections for our growth and communicate effectively with each of them. At this level we will be articulate and able to foster the give and take necessary for effective teamwork. And we may be able to simplify the infinite complexity we experience into a practical framework that others can use.

Like Elizabeth Kübler-Ross, a Swiss-born psychiatrist whose early experiences inspired her to dedicate her life to healing. In her first book, *On Death and Dying*, she pioneered psychological counselling to the dying through her now famous Five Stages of Grief - denial, anger, bargaining, depression, and acceptance. And she went on to become the author of 24 books published in 41 languages.

And at the spiritually evolved level, we will be able to invoke insight and inspire others. At this level we can facilitate group integration, enabling the group to act as an organic whole because we understand the culture in its rich detail. This insight gives us the ability to be in the right place at the right time and understand how best to maximize our growth and influence.

Like Jiddu Krishnamurti, who was discovered as a 14 year old in India by the Theosophical Society and groomed to be their next World Teacher. However, at age 34, he closed the order saying: *"Truth is a pathless land... I want to do a certain thing in the world and I am going to do it with unwavering concentration: to set man free. I desire to free him from all cages, from all fears, and not to found religions, new sects, nor to establish new theories and new philosophies."[13]* Yet he went on to tour the world and give talks until his death at age 91.

Fourth House

Makemake in the 4th House will open us to see the bigger personal picture and enable us to draw spirit into a sacred space in our home. With this placement we are able to nurture our roots and our psychological foundation through an infusion of spirit, and understand how our inner psychology connects with the organic whole of who we are.

Yet at the unconscious level, family issues and the conflicts, fears and dreams involved may play a large part in our world and we may get caught up in the drama, and not fully understand the consequences of our actions. If we feel that our inner emotional security is challenged, we may stop playing by the rules or cooperating with others, or we could be verbally deceptive or manipulative, or try to hide as a coping skill.

Like Amy Grossberg, a US teenager who hid her pregnancy from her family. Even after she and her boyfriend secretly birthed their baby boy in a motel, she refused to accept his existence. They put the child in a plastic bag and left him in a dumpster where he was later found and diagnosed as having been a live, healthy birth. He had died from multiple skull fractures and apparently from having been shaken. Grossberg blamed her boyfriend, pleaded for leniency and told the judge, *"I want to help others. I want to make a difference."*

---

13 https://www.jkrishnamurti.org/about-dissolution-speech#:~:text=I%20want%20to%20do%20a,new%20theories%20and%20new%20philosophies.

On the other hand, when we are on the spiritual path we can find the devotional focus to understand the rich tapestry of karmic lessons that each moment holds. At this level we know we are each a speck in the vast universe, but that the spirit energies can find us and nourish us when we are devoted and in the natural rhythm.

And at the spiritually evolved level, our complex understanding of the way the world works will gain the support of others, and we may become a master of a spiritual system which can connect with others on a soul level.

Like David Cochrane, a US astrologer whose empirical research in astrology and consultations with thousands of clients has formed the basis for his development of Vibrational Astrology. *"Astrology, like literature and art, enhances one's perspective and is edifying to the soul… This is why astrology has persisted through the ages. People do not cling to astrology because they are superstitious, gullible, and stupid. They cling to astrology for the same reason they cling to literature, art, and music; they lift the soul."*

Fifth House

With Makemake in the 5th House, we will be able to experiment creatively with our lives, taking the risks required to be ourselves in each moment and enjoy doing it. This is the house of creative self-expression and we are able to bring a devotional focus which permits extreme talent to this work, but this can come at the expense of neglecting other areas.

This is also the house of love affairs, and at the unconscious level we might engage in double talk to facilitate our sexual relationships, and be manipulative with our communication about our love. At this level we could also get involved in speculation or gambling, acting recklessly with a tendency to put short term advantage ahead of long term gain.

Like French exotic dancer and spy, Mata Hari. During the First World War her neutral status as a Dutch citizen enabled her to cross borders when the love of her life, a young Russian soldier, was wounded. However, this came at the cost of becoming a spy for France. She was tasked with seducing the Crown Prince of Germany and, to gain access, she offered him intelligence. As a result she was later accused of being a double agent for Germany, was arrested by the French and tried for treason, then executed by firing squad.

When we are on the spiritual path, however, we can learn to joyfully participate in the creative risks of being alive, and to work as part of a team to achieve common aspirations. This joyful participation will lead to a richer awareness and we might teach our passion.

Like American astrologer Philip Sedgwick, who is known for his Deep Space and Whole Sky astrology. A self-proclaimed researcher by nature, he compiled a Galactic Ephemeris of over 8,700 deep space objects. He has taught and presented internationally, and he uses comedy to communicate his heavenly messages. His books include *The Astrology of Transcendence*, and *The Astrology of Deep Space*.

At this spiritually evolved level, we are open to spirit and are learning to love unconditionally. At this level, we can see the bigger picture and are able to invoke insight and inspiration through our quick-witted creative work.

Sixth House

With Makemake in the 6th House, we will likely be clever and quick-witted as we go about our daily routine, or do our job. This is the house of health and physical sickness, and we have the ability to listen to ourselves and foster our wellness through appropriate responses in each moment. We can also use fast footwork in our response to everyday crises and are able to join with others and work as a team to achieve common aspirations.

At the unconscious level however, we might not see the advantage in this, and we may engage in double talk, where we say one thing and do another. Or we could play fast and loose with the facts to gain short term advantage, essentially not playing by the rules or cooperating with others.

Like conservative US media personality Sean Hannity, who, until recently was the highest paid Fox News anchor, and known for promoting "deep state" conspiracy theories. According to The Washington Post, Hannity *"repeatedly embraces storylines that prove to be inaccurate"* and takes positions on a range of topics that change over time.

When we are on the spiritual path however, we understand that the spirit energies can find us and nourish us, if we are devoted and in tune with ourselves. At this level we learn to call the nourishment of spirit into our lives through the services we perform.

Like former US Secretary of State, Condoleezza Rice, who grew up in Alabama while the U.S. South was still racially segregated, yet completed her Ph.D. in political science by the age of 26. She became the first female African-American US Secretary of State and the first woman to serve as national security advisor. She said of this time: *"To have a chance to serve my country as the nation's chief diplomat at a time of peril and consequence, that was enough."[14]*

And at the spiritually evolved level, we can embrace the divine in the rich tapestry of each moment of our lives. And we know that we'll get best results when we do it with an unflinching gaze and fierce grace that leaves no detail out. At this level everything becomes a valuable, creative resource for our growth, and we develop a devotional focus in our service to others.

Seventh House

With Makemake in the 7th House, our relationships bring us freedom, expansiveness, and connect us with spirit, opening us to see the bigger picture. With this placement we are articulate with those closest to us, and able to see through the legalese of contracts and all things official.

At the unconscious level, however, we could fall into backbiting and rivalry, quarreling with our partners, and engaging in double talk and manipulation to maintain our relationships. At this level we could also take flight to avoid the consequence of our actions, or develop enemies and become involved in lawsuits through our reckless and self-serving approach.

In the extreme, we can see Adolf Hitler, whose policies and promotion of the Holocaust inflicted human suffering on an unprecedented scale. Of the five women that he has been romantically connected to, three were roughly two decades younger than he, and only one lived a long life and died of natural causes. Two died by suicide, a third died of complications from her attempted suicide, and the fourth also attempted suicide.

---

14 https://www.azquotes.com/quote/654802

When we are on the spiritual path however, we begin to understand the give and take required for our relationships to work, and can develop the ability to work together as a team. At this level we understand that each relationship we have is perfect for our growth, and we learn to co-operate and be diplomatic with our significant others.

At the spiritually evolved level, we can develop cooperative partnerships and joyfully participate in them, conscious of the organic whole that is created by being together. At this level we have the devotional focus to appreciate the rich tapestry created by our network of relationships and can foster each of them.

Like the iconic talk show host Oprah Winfrey, who has garnered countless awards stemming from the reputation she built through her one-to-one relationships on The Oprah Winfrey Show. She is known as an empathic and authentic communicator who is able to draw out the rich tapestry of people's life stories, and make a strong connection with her audience. She has said: *"I have church with myself: I believe in the God force that lives inside all of us, and once you tap into that, you can do anything."*[15]

Eighth House

With Makemake in the 8th House, we understand how we interact with the collective energies in our lives to form an organic whole. This is the house of karma and this placement helps us feel the complex intermingling of karmic energies in each moment, tuning us into the bigger picture.

At the unconscious level however, we might act in a reckless and self-serving way with joint resources, which can lead

15 Lowe, Janet (January 22, 2001). Oprah Winfrey Speaks: Insights from the World's Most Influential Voice. John Wiley & Sons. p. 122. ISBN 978-0-471-39994-0.

to losses, debts or bankruptcy. At this level we might have to make personal sacrifices to facilitate the regeneration necessary in our lives.

Like American entrepreneur Martha Stewart who rose from a modest background to become the first female self-made billionaire. She was known as a shrewd, competitive and even ruthless businesswoman. However she committed insider trading to avoid losses of $50,000 and was subsequently indicted by a grand jury on nine counts, including charges of securities fraud and obstruction of justice.

However, when we are on the spiritual path we have the courage to experiment with the occult, and discover the rich tapestry of self-transformation possible in each moment. This is also the house of commitments of all kinds and at this level we will be competitive and best practice.

And at the spiritually evolved level we understand the cycle of death and rebirth. At this level we can see the big picture and can integrate this with our personal devotional focus at such a deep level, that we may have a clairvoyance about how things are playing out in our lives and what is to come.

Like American astrologer Steven Forrest, one of the founders of Evolutionary Astrology, which embraces paradigms and methodologies that specifically measure the growth of the soul from life to life. Asked about free will versus fate, he said, *"I am personally confident that we humans are capable of changing ourselves, capable of evolution. None of us is limited to a 'nature' that is cast in stone by the positions of the planets. As we change ourselves, we make different choices and thus create different futures."*[16]

16 Forrest, Steven (2012). Yesterday's Sky: Astrology and Reincarnation. Borrego Springs, CA: Seven Paws Press. pp. 24, 25, 340. ISBN 978-0-9790677-3-0.

Ninth House

With Makemake in the 9th House, we are interested in big thoughts and big ideas and we can experiment with them to gain a richer awareness. We are able to bring a devotional yet playful focus to this work, through which we can uncover the real meaning of things.

At the unconscious level however, religion might substitute for our individual research, providing the answers so we don't have to do the work ourselves. And this spiritual laziness could also lead us to develop questionable ethics and morals, engaging in double talk and playing loosely with the facts to support our alternate realities.

Like Julian Assange, an Australian hacker and activist who founded WikiLeaks. To avoid extradition on charges of sexual assault in Sweden, and conspiracy to commit computer intrusion in the US, he was given asylum for 7 years in the Ecuadorian Embassy in London. And, after a dispute with the embassy, he has since been held in a British prison for 4 years while his US extradition charges are disputed.

In an interview with the Sydney Morning Herald in 2010 he said: *"The sense of perspective that interaction with multiple cultures gives you I find to be extremely valuable, because it allows you to see the structure of a country with greater clarity, and gives you a sense of mental independence. You're not swept up in the trivialities of a nation. You can concentrate on the serious matters."*[17]

When we are on the spiritual path however, this placement is rich in the philosophies and the learning opportunities that we need for our growth. At this level we might be a bit of a spiritual

---

17 https://www.smh.com.au/national/keeper-of-secrets-20100521-w230.html

trickster, with an experimental, practice based approach to our search for spiritual meaning.

And at the spiritually evolved level, we can gain understanding and wisdom through our joyful participation in the process of taking old ideas and playing with them experimentally to liberate the active components.

Like astrologer Eleanor Bach, unsung champion of the asteroids, whose 1973 book *Ephemerides of the Asteroids* put Ceres, Pallas, Juno and Vesta on the astrological map. She paved the way for Demetra George's work representing *"new voices of the dormant feminine, recently activated and now demanding power, recognition, justice and equality in our society."*[18]

Tenth House

With Makemake in the 10th House, we will be communicative and self-assured in our professional work, and have a deep understanding of the culture or nation in which we are involved. We may take on a public speaking role, or get involved with training people or groups to operate in a social context.

At the unconscious level however, we could act in a reckless and self-serving way in our profession, or take flight to avoid the consequence of our professional actions. At this level we could also develop the ability to hide in plain sight as a coping skill, or try to overcompensate by hogging the limelight.

Like US industrialist John D Rockefeller Sr, who came from humble beginnings. He had such a keen eye for the long-term

18 George, Demetra, & Bloch, Douglas (2003). Asteroid Goddesses: The Mythology, Psychology, and Astrology. Nicolas-Hays, Inc. ISBN 9780892540822

role that petroleum would play in post-Civil War USA that his company Standard Oil monopolized 90% of the market until it was disbanded by a Supreme Court ruling. Rockefeller is still widely known as the richest person in modern history and the US's first billionaire.

When we are on the spiritual path, we can become socially responsible and find the devotional focus to understand the rich tapestry of our lives that each moment holds. This enables us to see what we can do to help society develop.

Like U.S. First Lady Betty Ford, who, as a result of her own journey with substance abuse and addictions to pain medicine and alcohol, established the Betty Ford Centre, thus bringing greater national awareness and acceptance to this closeted issue. By speaking candidly she helped to destigmatize this and other hot topics such as women's rights, gay rights, equal pay, abortion, breast cancer awareness, sex, drugs, and the HIV/AIDS crisis.

And at the spiritually evolved level, we can invoke insight and inspiration in others, and may become well known and receive honours through this work. At this level we can see the organic whole of the culture and also how we can most effectively play our part in it.

Eleventh House

With Makemake in the 11th House, we will be receptive to collective forces and seek out groups that can help us expand our consciousness. This is the house of our hopes and goals, and with this placement we can see the big picture and integrate this with our personal devotional focus so we can play our part in the collective.

At the unconscious level, however, our need to belong might lead us to get involved with groups that purport to be one thing and are actually something else. And at this level our ambition could also lead us to act recklessly and in a self-serving way in the groups that we are part of, not playing by the rules or cooperating with others.

Like U.S. financier Bernie Madoff who was found guilty of having defrauded about 37,000 investors across 136 countries of billions of dollars over his forty year career. As the mastermind of the largest Ponzi scheme in history, at the age of seventy he was sentenced to 150 years in prison and died there twelve years later.

When we are on the spiritual path however, we can adopt a more charitable attitude and joyfully participate in the self-realization that is possible in this house. At this level the give and take of teamwork in the groups to which we belong, brings a richer awareness and opens us to see the bigger picture.

Like renowned artist and civil rights activist, Maya Angelou, who had a difficult childhood. She was raped at age eight by her stepfather, who was later killed for his crime, causing her to go mute for 5 years, fearing the immense power of her words. When her first memoir *I Know Why the Caged Bird Sings* was published, it was a watershed not only for her, but for women and for Black people. Although known for her 7 autobiographies that bend the genre, her life itself was her art.

At this spiritually evolved level, we can adopt a loving approach to our community, drawing spirit into our lives in the process. At this level we can play with our interaction with the collective consciousness to liberate the active components and create new collective awareness.

Twelfth House

With Makemake in the 12th House, we are involved in a deep investigation of our subconscious and also of the collective unconscious of the culture in which we live. With this placement we can bring a devotional focus to our subconscious habit patterns that come from the past, to understand how they underpin the rich tapestry of each moment.

This is the house of the self that we don't show to others and, at the unconscious level, we might double down on this by developing an ability to hide in plain sight as a coping skill. At this level we could also become involved with secret relationships and engage in double lives.

Like Arnold Schwarzenegger, who is widely known as a Hollywood actor and in later years became governor of California. However his 25 year marriage to Maria Shriver of the Kennedy family ended when he admitted to fathering a child with their long-time housemaid at the same time as their fourth child was on the way. The affair was kept secret for thirteen years until the housekeeper brought her son to work one day.

When we are on the spiritual path however, we can practice self-sacrifice and forgiveness, and through this release our karmic debts and heal our subconscious wounds. At this level we value seclusion as a means to connect with the divine, and we understand that we are each a speck in the vast universe, yet the spirit energies can find us and nourish us, if we are devoted and in the natural rhythm.

At the spiritually evolved level, we will always be in the right place at the right time for our consciousness growth. At this level we are connected to the divine in each moment and may experience revelations or miracles.

Like social reformer and feminist, Annie Besant, who championed women's rights, and workers' rights. She was the first woman to promote birth control, for which she was arrested. Annie also advocated freedom of thought and was a prolific speaker and writer. When she was forty three she became head of the Theosophical Society and remained president until her death 26 years later. In this role she was instrumental in discovering and grooming Jiddu Krishnamurti to be the next "World Teacher."

Workbook to Onboard Makemake in Your Life

1. Work out where Makemake is in your birth chart:

    a. Go to www.astro.com and create a free account.

    b. Then choose "Extended Chart Selection" under "Charts & Data" and put in your birth data.

    c. On this data screen, at the bottom on the left under 'Additional Objects', you can choose to include the dwarfs, which are listed as Asteroids, and you do this by highlighting them. The dwarfs in this box are *Ceres, Eris, Ixion, Orcus, Quaoar, Sedna & Varuna.*

    d. Then opposite this, in the box on the bottom right, add these numbers (**136108,136472, 225088, 120347**) to also include *Haumea, Makemake, Gonggong & Salacia.*

    e. Click 'Show the Chart' to see it.

    f. Then click 'Additional Tables' at the top left of the chart to get the table of positions and aspects.

2. Look up the house interpretation in this book for your house placement and see what resonates.

3. What does the Sabian Symbol for your Makemake indicate to you? Search online for Dane Rudhyar's or Marc Edmund Jones's interpretations. (Remember to round up to find the right symbol, i.e. 22.04 = 23).

4. Next, understand how Makemake interacts with the other planets in your chart by studying the aspects. I.e. – is Makemake conjunct, opposite, trine, square or sextile any of your personal planets or points like Sun, Moon, Ascendant, Mercury, Venus, Ceres, Mars, Jupiter or Saturn? How about the transpersonal planets like Uranus, Neptune, Pluto, Ixion, Orcus, Salacia, Quaoar, Makemake, Gonggong, Eris and Sedna?

5. Choose a significant moment of understanding in your life and look up the transits of Pluto and Saturn to your natal Makemake on that date. You can find the list of where these two planets on this ephemeris: https://www.astro.com/swisseph/swepha_e.htm. And then check the Makemake transits to your other natal planet. You can find the Makemake ephemeris at this link: https://www.astro.com/swisseph/makemake.htm.

6. Given what you've learned so far, write a couple of paragraphs on how can you best activate Makemake in your life?

Makemake in our New Firmament

The outer planets represent aspects of consciousness. We have become familiar with Uranus, Neptune and Pluto, and over the early years of this century we have discovered 10 new planets who offer us a rich feast of new consciousness. Let's look at each of these outer planets to put them in context.

As we embark on the spiritual path to make a larger sense out of the experiences of our personal lives, we start activating our Uranian and Neptunian energies and bring them into our consciousness. As we do, we begin to realize that the 'you can't take it with you" approach of the inner planets is actually a delusion.

Uranus brings intuitive flashes into our personal planet consciousness and begins to connect us with the collective consciousness, breaking through our Saturnian defenses to allow new impulses and connections. So, the discovery of Uranus enabled consciousness growth in our lives. We can look at Uranus as the higher octave of Mercury because he takes Mercury's ideas, communications and curiosity, and networks them at a higher spiritual level.

Neptune tunes us into the bigger picture and brings spiritual consciousness into our lives. He encourages us to search for a larger meaning for our personal experiences and teaches us about faith as a way of deepening consciousness. Neptune is traditionally considered to be the higher octave of Venus, where the inner planet's values and aesthetics are expressed at a more spiritual level through the imagination and psychic opening of Neptune.

Which brings us to dwarf planet **Pluto**, who is the start of the outer transpersonal planets. Here we must accept the limitations of the ego consciousness, let go of compulsions and unconscious constructs and accept that change is the only constant. Pluto is traditionally considered to be the higher octave of Mars.

The discovery of Pluto enabled the psychological understanding of our lives. This produced the shadow paradigm, where the darkness in our souls is seen to be buried in our unconscious, and the convenience of this is that we don't have to address it on a day-to-day basis. But we need to ditch Pluto's shadow paradigm to enable him and these other new energies consciously in our lives. As with all the other outer planets, Pluto manifests differently depending on our level of consciousness, so what we have been calling his shadow is simply his manifestation when we are at personal planet consciousness.

As we get on the spiritual path, Pluto gives us an adaptability and resilience which enables us to mediate the transition occurring in our lives in each moment. And at the spiritually evolved level, we can transmute loneliness and separation into love and long-term relationships and effect a regeneration in our lives.

Pluto now has two new brothers who share his orbit and his angle to the ecliptic. They also share his gravitational resonance with Neptune, as all three do two orbits of the Sun, to every three of Neptune's. These brothers are however polar opposites.

The first is **Ixion**, who encourages us to be a passionate, but lawless, follower of our heart, or loins, depending on our consciousness level. He's always asking the question: 'are the rules we're playing by the right ones?' And he does this by pushing the boundaries and asking for forgiveness afterwards, rather than permission before. As we develop a spiritual approach, we can learn to honor the bad girl or bad boy energy inside us and follow our heart. At this level Ixion encourages us to be an independent and unique expression of ourselves, while being sensitive to the unspoken agreements in our relationships, so we know how far we can go.

The second is Pluto's straight-talking brother, **Orcus**. He is the master of integrity at the highest level, but he also encourages us to engage in double-talk and deception at the personal planet level. Yet as we develop spiritually he gives us a self-sufficiency that will nourish us through the long and difficult work that we sometimes find necessary, plus a capacity to deal with the shadow side of our lives. At this level we become accountable for our deeds and actions. We learn to align with a spiritual creed and understand the karmic process of life. And, at the highest level, we gain the shamanic ability to transmute shadow into light.

Next, we have **Salacia**, who gives us a self-protective quality that helps us weather the real and psychic storms. She can give us the power to foresee opportunities, and find the appropriate time to embrace them. She enables us to take a leap of faith, especially when we know we are going to be profoundly transformed by the experience. At the personal planet level there can be erotic fascination or interest, and socially unacceptable, often illicit, sexual activity. And in challenging or difficult aspects, we might feel not in control or unable to change a situation. At the highest level, however, Salacia is about bringing true love into our lives and empowering us spiritually.

Then we have **Varuna**, who is the higher octave of Saturn. Where Saturn rules by control and through laws and restriction, Varuna has a natural sovereignty, but we have to claim this through action. Sovereignty is a dance between our intention and the collective psyche. We have to claim it and at the same time others have to agree to give it to us. We start this process by stepping forth in some way and saying 'I can do this'. And then we have to keep doing it over time. And, when we do, we gain support and notability for this work. Once we are on the spiritual path, Varuna teaches us to stand in the center of our lives and own the results of our dance of karma and dharma.

As we move further out from the Sun, we find **Haumea**, who is a creation deity of the Hawaiian people. She is both an earth goddess and a fire goddess, and she represents regeneration and rebirth. She is the higher octave of Neptune, turning his psychic opening into real psychic connection. At the personal planet level however, this can manifest as a lack of connection, a sort of spiritual alienation. As we develop spiritually, she provides a link with the oneness of humanity, with the magic of being alive. So, she represents a direct link with the soul level when we can open ourselves to it.

Just beyond Haumea, we have our first non-gendered planet, **Quaoar**, the creation deity of the Tongva people, who are indigenous to Los Angeles. Quaoar sings and dances the world into existence, so this planet talks about a practice of bringing spirit into matter. Singing and dancing are practices that bring spirit into matter, and so are yoga, meditation, walking in the woods, and many other things. Anything can be a practice to bring spirit into our lives. We can look at Quaoar as the higher octave of Jupiter. Where Jupiter is a sort of dumb luck, Quaoar turns each moment into a dynamic meditation where we can see the opportunities and act on them in real time, so Quaoar is like smart luck.

Our next planet is **Makemake**, who is the higher octave of Uranus. Makemake takes Uranus's intuitive network and talks about the rich context that it addresses, about the culture, or the nation that is created as a result. At the personal planet level, we might use this rich intuitive understanding to hide in plain sight, to blend into the background as a safety mechanism. As we develop spiritually however, he calls spiritual nourishment into our lives and gives us a devotional focus bordering on genius.

This is followed by **Gonggong**, who is a Chinese water god. He is an empathic wizard at the highest level, able to feel inside other people and walk a mile in their shoes. We have to get out of our own emotions to empathize with others however, so at the personal planet level, he can be a bit of an enfant terrible, encouraging us to be very emotionally self-indulgent and to lash out in an attempt to get our own way. As we develop spiritually, we can lift our energy out of our personal space and empathize with others. Empathy allows us to motivate others from the inside, to combine our energies and lift the spiritual vibe.

Next we have **Eris**, who is the warrior sister of Mars in myth. And we know that Pluto is the higher octave of Mars, so Eris is the higher octave of Pluto. She shines her fierce grace on everything in our lives, seeking inclusion and validation for all the disparate facets of our psyche. At the personal planet level, she encourages us to engage in discord and strife, so we learn to stop fooling ourselves, or stop being fooled. But as we adopt a more spiritual approach, she enables us to see clearly without preconceptions and keep our body and mind in harmony so that health and happiness prevails. And at the highest level she is a spirit-guide, transmuting life into love.

And finally, we have the new outer limit of our solar system, **Sedna**, who is always trying to get us onto the spiritual path.

She represents *Our Soul's Path of Destiny* because, if we accept that our soul incarnates over a number of lifetimes and that it has a purpose to grow through these incarnations, then in this life, that purpose is shown by the Sedna placement.

We can think of Sedna as the higher octave of **Ceres**, who is our newly reclassified inner dwarf planet, orbiting between Mars and Jupiter. Ceres is our ability to love and be loved. At both a basic level and in the bigger sense of the word, she represents what we need to feed and nourish ourselves. We can think of Ceres as the higher octave of the Moon. The Moon is our heart center, the other luminary in our chart, where we see ourselves reflected in each moment. The Moon mediates our survival through each of those moments and Ceres talks of the process of those moments and mediates our survival over time.

Sedna steps this heart-centered energy all the way out to the new limit of our solar system, so she talks of our survival over lifetimes. Here we learn to let go of the physical realm and allow transcendence to a new holistic spiritual consciousness where we can allow love and harmony, and nurture abundance.

Dwarf Planets as Higher Octaves

Here is a framework of higher octaves to help us understand several of the dwarf planets. A higher octave expresses an inner planet energy at a more spiritual level. But Dane Rudhyar reminds us in the below quote from Horoscope Magazine, that the higher octaves act on the lower octaves to repolarize and transform them. (The planets in bold are dwarf planets).

Sedna - **Ceres** - Moon

Haumea – Neptune – Venus

Makemake – Uranus – Mercury

Eris – **Pluto** – Mars

Quaoar – Jupiter

Varuna - Saturn

When Uranus, Neptune and Pluto are considered as "higher" expressions of such planets as Mercury, Venus and Mars… the closer planets are seen to represent a "lower octave" of biological-personal functions or energies; the more remote ones, beyond Saturn, a "higher octave" constituted of more transcendent and "spiritual" activities or qualities of being.

There is some truth, no doubt, in such statements if one restricts oneself to a consideration of only the external events of a person's life. The "illuminations" which Uranus may bring to the consciousness that is not frozen into Saturnian rigidity can inspire and transform the Mercury mind. The compassion and inclusiveness which are characteristic of Neptune do act directly — if allowed by Saturn so to act—upon the sense of value and the feeling-judgments represented by Venus. The power of inescapable destiny and total surrender to a cause, which defines essentially Pluto's operations, do transform — if allowed to do so — the strictly personal initiative of Mars.

But the essential fact is that the activities of Uranus, Neptune and Pluto run counter to the normal functions of Mercury, Venus and Mars. The former are not just personal activities of a "higher" kind; they are activities meant to disturb and transform — indeed, utterly to repolarize and reorient those of Mercury, Venus and Mars.[19]

---

19 https://www.khaldea.com/rudhyar/astroarticles/planetaryoctaves. php

Dwarf Planet University

The information in this book comes out of research at the Dwarf Planet University, where we are pioneering the astrological exploration of the Kuiper Belt. The dwarf planets speak of new aspects of consciousness that are arising in our lives, and we offer 6 week courses to on-board each of them.

The courses explore the planets in our personal chart and the charts of the other class members. We look at the house placement and the aspects and research our transits, as we understand how to on-board each aspect of consciousness.

The course format mixes webinars, blog-posted assignments and live Zoom Q&As, so you can attend from anywhere in the world. We start with a live Welcome Q&A and we explore the House position in the first fortnight, the aspects in the second and transits in the third. Each fortnight includes an instructional webinar, an investigative assignment based on our personal chart and a live 2 hour Zoom Q&A session.

Assignments are posted on a private forum so we can learn from, and comment on, posts from our fellow course members. And the live Q&A sessions are recorded so we can pick up classes we miss.

The students on our courses range from beginners to very experienced astrologers, and it is this range that is the source of the vibrant class culture. What students love is the community sharing that occurs, through the blog-posted assignments and live Zoom Q&As, which gives a good picture of how these new planets act similarly, and yet diversely, in each of our lives.

We offer a Dwarf Planet Astrology Diploma on completion of any 8 of our 11 courses, but you are also welcome to do courses singly and in any order, and all the courses have a mix of ongoing and casual students.

Community Program

We also offer a Community Program which is designed for those who want to explore these new aspects of consciousness, but don't want to commit to assignments and in-depth study.

As a community participant you get a copy of your chart including the dwarfs, and also get access to all 11 on-demand webinars which introduce each dwarf planet. These include the house interpretations, which is where we see these outer planets manifesting most clearly in our lives. These webinars are posted throughout the year, just prior to the start of each course.

You also have the opportunity to participate in four Zoom gatherings throughout the year where Uni founder, Alan Clay, will talk about the current dwarf transits, answer questions and look at example charts.

What Students Say:

I highly recommend the Dwarf Planets Course for the insights and the amount of new information and perspective gathered. Alan's teaching inspires one and brings new light and spiritual understanding to charts (certainly to mine). His humor and friendly approach made the seminars very enjoyable yet profound.

Elisabetta Quintiliani, Astrologer - Italy

Alan Clay's sensitive, cutting edge wisdom and the community sharing make the classes on the Dwarf Planets compelling and profound. They are as much an exploration as a revelation. Not only mentally stimulating, they are a deep dive into each of our psyche and growth experience. I love them and am looking forward to more.

Karen La Puma, Astrologer, Counselor, Speaker.

I'm very grateful for Alan Clay's insightfully powerful dwarf planet courses. He offers a supportive and welcoming class environment that encourages learning and processing the deep new consciousness of these planets. I totally recommend engaging into this outer realm of alchemy into our inner self!

Sue Rose Minahan, Evolutionary Post-Modern Astrologer

What Alan Clay has created with the Dwarf Planet University is nothing short of genius. His in-depth knowledge and amazing teaching style are unique and what the astrological world has been waiting for. I'm so enjoying learning about our far reaching dwarf planets amongst a galaxy of friendly, intelligent student astrologers from all over the universe, logging on at their differing time zones.

Eileen Richardson, UK.

Alan Clay's work has transformed my thinking—about my chart, about my practice—even about astrology itself. Alan is a born teacher. -

Ariel Harper Nave, Canada

I absolutely loved the class! As a first time student of astrology, I can honestly say that aside from Alan (a wonderful teacher and guide), every one of the students in the class was a teacher for me. I learned so much and can't wait for the next class to begin. -

Mary Anne Pitt, USA

Who would have thought that studying the dwarf planets would lead to such an expansive awareness of my soul's journey? For this, I am very grateful. The style and structure of Alan's teaching provide the group with a very warm, safe and informative space in which to learn. I love being part of the group. Thank you, Alan. -

Marian Ryan, Energy Therapist, Author, Teacher, UK

Meet the Writers

New Zealander **Alan Clay** is a transpersonal astrologer, specialising in the outer planets, and inspired by the work of Dane Rudhyar. Over the years this has broadened into a study of the new dwarf planets, and today he is one of the Kuiper Belt's astrological pioneers.

Alan worked for many years internationally as a clown and a clown teacher, which he describes as being a big research into people and what makes us human. And he combined this with consulting astrology work to explore the depths or our psyche.

He is well known for his clown textbook, *Angels Can Fly*, which includes a mix of clown theory, workshop and street exercises, anecdotes from 20 international clowns, and fictional stories following the adventures of 10 street clowns.

He is also the writer and director of an award winning romantic comedy film, *Courting Chaos*, in which a Beverly Hills girl falls for a Venice Beach street clown called Chaos, and she must overcome her inhibitions and become a clown herself for the relationship to survive.

His book, *Sedna Consciousness, the Soul's Path of Destiny* was launched at UAC 2018 in Chicago. It is the ultimate reference on the new outer limit of our solar system, the planet Sedna. The book includes aspect interpretations with all the traditional planets, as well as all the new dwarf planets.

Following several years of teaching dwarf planet astrology courses online, Alan founded the Dwarf Planet University under the Jupiter/Saturn conjunction in 2000. Since then he has developed all the course material that is used by students at the Uni, and he leads the fortnightly live Zoom Q&As. He still works as a consulting astrologer and is available for chart readings by Zoom.

Melissa Elvira Billington is the child of a healer and a physicist, conceived in a conscientious objector's community in Nova Scotia but born in Virginia and raised in the Northeastern US. She worked in the arts in Santa Fe, Boise, and New York City before heading to India in 1999 for the last full solar eclipse of the last millennium.

As the stars would have it, she has lived and worked as an artist and yoga teacher in India, Barbados, Puerto Rico, New Zealand, and now Australia. She has studied dwarf planet astrology with Alan for five years and worked as an assistant teacher at the Dwarf Planet Uni for the last two.

Here is her first spiritual work, age 7, fresh from the ashram:

Inner and Outer space

is a wondrous place

to be at peace with yourself.

Love is the peace of mind

that binds us together

in outer and inner space as one.

www.ingramcontent.com/pod-product-compliance
Lightning Source LLC
Chambersburg PA
CBHW050014090426
42734CB00020B/3270